WATERBIRDS

WATERBIRDS

BIRDS OF SOUTHERN AFRICA'S WETLANDS

PHOTOGRAPHY BY NIGEL DENNIS ~ TEXT BY WARWICK TARBOTON

Dedicated to David Skead and Koos Geldenhuys who were tragically killed
while conducting an aerial census of waterfowl on the pans in the
northern Orange Free State on 16 October 1983.

Warwick Tarboton

First published in the UK in 1993 by
New Holland (Publishers) Ltd
37 Connaught Street, London W2 2AZ

ISBN 1 85368 258 6

Editor: Phillida Brooke Simons
Designer: René Greeff
Phototypeset by Diatype cc
Reproduction by Unifoto (Pty) Ltd
Printed and bound by Leefung-Asco Printers Ltd, Hong Kong

Nigel Dennis's photographs are marketed in the UK and Europe
by the Natural History Photographic Library, High Street, Ardingly, Sussex.

HALF-TITLE PAGE: *Malachite Kingfisher*
TITLE PAGE: *Spurwinged Goose*
OPPOSITE: *Dabchick*

Contents

The Ethiopian Snipe's mottled brown and buff plumage is designed to conceal it from predators in its marshy habitat. But, as seen above, when it ventures into open water, the benefits of its cryptic plumage are lost. It searches for food by touch rather than sight, probing its long beak deep into soft mud in search of small organisms.

ACKNOWLEDGEMENTS

MANY THANKS TO ALL the following people for their invaluable assistance, be it in the form of transport (by boat, aeroplane or fourwheel drive), accommodation, permission to work in reserves and on privately-owned land, or advice on finding some of the more elusive waterbird species that appear in this book:

Anthony Bannister, Peter Cloete, Brian and Betty Dennis, Jan and Eileen Drotsky, Clem Haagner, Ian Hulley, John Matterson, Keith Morgan, the Natal Parks Board (including Joanne Hayes, David Johnson, Martin Harvey, Roger de la Harpe, Peter Kertland and Trevor Scheepers), John and Theresa Nicolaides, OFS Conservation (Frans de Villiers, Wilton and Sonja Raats), Nigel Robson, Derek van Rensberg, Schalk van der Sandt, Marius van Zyl, Daphne Wilmot-Hildebrandt, Tim Wright and the staff of the Umgeni Valley Project and Pete and Marian Zeeman.

Thanks to Tony Girling and the staff of Photoworld, Durban (surely the friendliest and most professional photo store in the country) and to Citylab, Durban, for their care in film processing.

Special thanks go to Tim Harris (NHPA, England) and to Lesley Hay and Barbara Bannister (ABPL, Lanseria) for their encouragement and assistance over the years and for allowing me access to some of my transparencies in their files for use in this project. Similarly, thanks to John Hone (Art Publishers, Durban) and John Kaprielian (Photo Researchers, New York) for use of my pictures from their files.

I am most grateful to Warwick Tarboton for providing direction as to the photographic content of *Waterbirds* plus, of course, for such a comprehensive and engaging text. Warwick's depth of knowledge and understanding of ornithology, along with his commitment to conservation, is an inspiration to us all.

My sincere appreciation goes to the Struik staff for their enthusiasm and commitment in the production of *Waterbirds*, in particular Eve Gracie, Peter Borchert and René Greeff.

Lastly, very special thanks go to my wife Wendy, whose companionship on all the numerous photographic expeditions greatly enhanced the magic and wonder of the natural world. Much of the past year has been spent camping in wilderness areas where, in addition to having to share a campsite with snakes, scorpions and grazing hippos, Wendy has also had to tolerate an occasionally bad-tempered photographer when the waterbirds proved uncooperative!

Nigel Dennis
Merrivale
May 1993

*Ungainly in flight, the African Spoonbill (above) appears front-heavy with its
outstretched neck and long, spatulate bill. This is virtually the only time one hears
this species utter its husky, grunting call. Like other waterbirds, large groups of
spoonbills often fly in V-formation: each bird apparently uses less energy flying in
another's slipstream, and leadership is rotated between members of the group.*

PHOTOGRAPHER'S PREFACE

MY PHOTOGRAPHY USUALLY includes the broadest spectrum of natural subjects, but gradually the idea of a book specifically on southern African waterbirds emerged. Such exquisite creatures living in an environment of subtle colours and reflections certainly had the potential for an interesting project and I hoped that it would be possible to produce a book which would be pleasing to look at while also portraying the subject's behaviour and interaction with their habitat.

Hides of various kinds were used for most of the photography. At times one consisting of two floats covered by a miniature camouflaged domed tent proved very useful. A monopod was included in the structure as a firm camera-support. This strange contraption could be moved slowly into position by wading in shallow water or, in deeper water, by poling or paddling from the inside. After working in an area for several days, I often found that the birds became accustomed to this 'pile of rubbish' following them and would go about their business of feeding or display and courtship undeterred. In areas with large crocodiles or hippos, an aluminium-hulled boat with a hide built on top of it was used for obvious reasons. Although the floating hide worked well for some species (particularly herons, kingfishers and ibises), it proved useless for wary birds living in open pans. Here I had to use a static hide which it was usually necessary to set up some days before starting to take pictures.

A small proportion of photographs in *Waterbirds* made use of captive subjects. This was mostly done where I felt that particularly sensitive species were best left alone in the wild. Some species are so wary that it is really only possible to obtain satisfactory pictures at the nest. I do not enjoy nest photography because of the risk of disturbance or even desertion. For this reason, the few nest pictures were taken in situations where I was certain that there would be no risk of disruption to the bird's breeding.

There is considerable interest among the wildlife photographic community regarding the camera or lenses that a particular photographer is using and I sometimes feel that the importance of such things is overplayed. The most important factor in a good photograph is getting the subject to behave naturally in a situation where lighting and background are favourable. Having said that, I am aware that there have been some significant advances in technology in recent years that have increased the scope and quality of photography. I used three lenses while working on *Waterbirds*: a 600 mm F4, a 300 mm F2.8 and a 100–300 mm F5.6 zoom. All are manufactured by Canon and incorporate their 'L' series special optics with exceptional resolution and saturation. At times a matched 1.4X Canon teleconverter was used with the 600 mm and 300 mm lenses and gave little discernible reduction in image quality. All the lenses have autofocus with the two larger lenses incorporating Canon's fast and almost silent Ultrasonic system. With practice, one can obtain action and behaviour sequences impossible with manual focusing. Fujichrome Velvia was used almost exclusively. Velvia is a difficult film to shoot because of its slow speed and limited exposure latitude but when conditions are right it has an unparalleled sharpness and colour. On the few occasions when a faster film was required I used Fujichrome 100 or Kodachrome 64. As I frequently had to work in several centimetres of water, a Benbo tripod was employed. In addition to having waterproof legs, the Benbo is sturdy enough to support a big lens.

I spent 14 months working on the photography for *Waterbirds* and when I look back on the project, I shall always remember many special moments. To see a thousand White Pelicans systematically fishing a pan was a grand spectacle. A pair of Pied Kingfishers became so used to my floating hide that they would regularly perch a couple of centimetres above my head. If I looked behind me there was a good chance that an enterprising Spoonbill would be standing waiting for me to make my next move as my slow wading inside the hide stirred up its food. And just once, after a week of waiting, countless Lesser Flamingos surrounded me, bathing and preening. I hope that we shall learn to cherish and conserve our wetland areas so that future generations will also be able to experience such delights.

From Flamingos
to Flufftails

*Invariably gregarious, Lesser Flamingos gather in
their hundreds, thousands, and even millions, to feed
on microscopic algae that abound in many shallow
saline lakes and pans. Here birds are drinking from a
freshwater seep in such a pan. Their dark bills,
smaller size and richer-coloured plumage distinguish
Lesser from Greater Flamingos. Birds in breeding
condition show the most intense coloration.*

From Flamingos
to Flufftails

THERE IS NOTHING ORDINARY about waterbirds. Not only do many of them have extraordinary lifestyles or unusual habits but some provide us with the most dramatic spectacles that the natural world has to offer. Sometimes it is the sight of their sheer numbers that is so marvellous, or it may be the dazzle of their colour, or the urgency and clamour of their comings and goings. A million flamingos gathered to breed on Makgadikgadi Pan or half a million Redbilled Teal rising from Lake Ngami must surely rank among the most breathtaking wildlife spectacles of the world. Sometimes it is the images they project – the ringing call of the African Fish Eagle evocative of untamed wilderness; the cheering whistles of the echelons of Whitefaced Ducks that cross the night sky as they wing their way from one wetland to another, or the eerie hoot of an invisible flufftail from the depths of a marsh. Sometimes it is simply the patience or ingenuity that waterbirds display in acquiring the day's meal that is so amazing or the fascinating intrigue of their social life.

This book's first aim is to illustrate a cross-section of southern Africa's diverse assemblage of waterbirds. Secondly, it aims to provide some insight into their varied lifestyles, their habitats and their changing circumstances. It does not, however, pretend to be a comprehensive review of any of these topics. It covers the waterbirds found in southern Africa only – that region lying south of the Zambezi and Kunene rivers – though most of these species also occur elsewhere in Africa and some are found on other continents as well.

The term 'waterbird' is a vague one which may be defined according to one's particular aim. There is no definitive list of what species constitute the waterbirds: they are simply those birds that depend on aquatic environments for their livelihood. Implicit in the term is the fact that the bird obtains its food from an aquatic habitat. Many birds roost at night in trees or reeds over water because of the safety of these sites, or they come to water to drink: they are not waterbirds. Some bird families, like ducks, pelicans and flamingos, are unquestionably waterbirds; other families, like plovers and cranes, cannot be classed as waterbirds *en bloc* since they include aquatic, partially aquatic and non-aquatic species. Often, for convenience more than for any other reason, the term 'waterbird' is restricted to the aquatic species in the families that fall (taxonomically) between the grebes and skimmers, thus excluding smaller species like kingfishers and wagtails. The term 'waterbird' is also usually restricted to species that frequent inland rather than marine waters, but these cut-offs are open to anyone's interpretation or whim. We have excluded marine and coastal birds from our selection but have extended it to include the kingfishers, warblers and wagtails that depend on aquatic habitats for their survival. In all, 170 species which accord with our definition are found in southern Africa and these constitute perhaps 15 per cent of the world's waterbird species. About half are illustrated and described in the pages that follow.

From pelicans to pratincoles, flamingos to flufftails, the waterbirds are about as diverse an assemblage of birds as one can find. The only trait shared by many of them is their dependence on aquatic habitats and the nature of this dependence is almost as diverse as the species themselves. In southern Africa there are 28 bird families that include waterbird species (or 23 families if the narrower definition of grebes to skimmers is taken). Most of the world's waterbird families are represented here to a greater or lesser degree – grebes, cormorants, the Darter, herons, the Hamerkop, storks, ibises and spoonbills, flamingos, ducks and geese (although there are no true geese in southern Africa), the family Rallidae (which includes rails, moorhens and others), cranes, finfoots, the various

*Flamingos are filter feeders. They sift food particles from water which they suck
in with the beak held slightly open (opposite, Greater Flamingo). Then, with the beak
closed, they pump the water out, forcing it through the fine lamellae between the
upper and lower mandibles. Long legs enable flamingos to wade in deep water as this
Greater Flamingo (above) demonstrates. In even deeper water they feed by
swimming with the aid of their duck-like webbed feet.*

The yellow eye, black beak and bright orange legs distinguish the male
Cape Shoveller (above) from the drabber female. This is one of the few duck species
that is endemic to southern Africa. Fond of shallow pans, it feeds by swimming
slowly forward, filtering food particles from the water with its long,
partly-submerged, spatulate beak.

families making up the waders (plovers, jacanas, scolopacids and others), gulls, terns and skimmers and finally the few waterbird species found among the owls, kingfishers, swallows, warblers and wagtails. Southern Africa's full complement of waterbirds is listed in the Appendix on pages 130–133.

Nearly two-thirds of the region's waterbirds belong to five large, successful families. The first of these, ducks and geese (family Anatidae), includes 147 species worldwide, of which 16 occur in southern Africa as breeding residents and three as occasional vagrants from the Northern Hemisphere. In addition, two alien species (Mute Swan, Mallard) have been partially successful in establishing feral populations as a result of artificial introductions. It is curious that southern Africa does not support a greater diversity of ducks and geese: less than half the number of species found in North America or Europe occur here. However, two species, the South African Shelduck and Cape Shoveller, are endemic to the region; only one other waterbird has this distinction. No true geese occur in southern Africa; the Egyptian Goose is, in fact, a shelduck most closely related to the South African Shelduck, while the tiny Pygmy Goose and huge Spurwinged Goose are both so-called 'perching ducks', a relationship they share with the Knobbilled Duck. As their name implies, they often perch in trees and two of the three are obligatory tree-hole nesting species. The Spurwinged Goose sometimes nests in a tree hole but more usually on the ground or over water like most other ducks.

The adult male Knobbilled Duck derives its common name from a fleshy growth which it sports on the upper side of its beak. The bird shown below feeding on water lily tubers is a non-breeding male; at the start of the breeding season the knob becomes greatly enlarged. At a glance, these ducks appear to be black and white but a closer look reveals the black to be a shimmer of iridescent purple and green.

The main group of southern African ducks consists of what are known as 'dabbling ducks': Yellowbilled Duck, African Black Duck, Cape Teal, Hottentot Teal, Redbilled Teal and Cape Shoveller are the species involved. They are all relatively dull-plumaged species and the sexes show little or no colour difference. They obtain most of their food by dabbling and upending in the water and they feed to varying degrees on both vegetable and animal material. They all make a raucous quacking, the females being responsible for most of the noise while the males are more subdued. Another group of three species (Fulvous Duck, Whitefaced Duck and Whitebacked Duck) comprises the 'whistling ducks' and the delightful, three-syllabled whistle of the Whitefaced Duck is a characteristic sound of most tropical African wetlands. Fulvous Ducks utter a less melodious two-syllabled whistle and the Whitebacked Duck just scrapes into the group with its odd-sounding 'woo, WHEEoo'. Fulvous and Whitefaced Ducks are mainly tropical species that do not range very far south of Zululand. They often occur in large flocks, either found loafing on the shoreline showing their long legs and long necks, or swimming in the shallows in rafts while upending and diving for submerged plants and corms. The Whitebacked Duck bears little similarity to them; it lives its hunchbacked life on the water, diving for virtually all its food and scarcely ever setting foot on shore. The most specialized diving duck in southern Africa is the Maccoa, another small, hunchbacked bird that is very seldom seen out of water. It is southern Africa's only representative of the group known as 'stifftails'. Both male and female have a long, stiff tail which, when they are loafing, is held up at a 45° angle. Often in these circumstances their heads are tucked away out of sight and only their characteristic long, erect tails serve to identify them. There are several other peculiarities that make them unusual, one being their dimorphic plumage; another that the male has both a breeding and a non-breeding (or eclipse) plumage.

The Southern Pochard is somewhat similar to the Maccoa Duck in that males are more brightly coloured than females and both species have dark heads and blue beaks. This species' most striking feature is its strong, fast flight; when disturbed it rises straight up from the water (usually uttering its nasal squawk as it does), climbs steeply and flies like a rocket. There have been numerous recoveries of southern African-ringed Pochards which demonstrate that it is a wide-ranging traveller although, unlike the Knobbilled Duck, it does not cross the equator during such excursions. Birds ringed in the Transvaal have been recovered in Tanzania, Malawi, Kenya and Zambia and many others have been found closer to home. One ringed at Barberspan in the western Transvaal was recovered only seven days later in Mozambique, 747 kilometres away, shot by a hunter. All the southern African ducks move widely about the subcontinent although only the Pochard, the Knobbilled Duck and the Redbilled Teal move thousands, instead of simply hundreds, of kilometres. Their movements reflect the changing availability of habitat and bear little resemblance to the regular migrations undertaken by waterfowl on other continents, or by some of the other waterbird families represented in southern Africa which breed in one area and spend the non-breeding period in another. Instead, they are here today, gone tomorrow, building up in numbers on one wetland, abandoning another; breeding in some years, missing others.

The Rallidae, consisting of rails, crakes, flufftails, gallinules, moorhens and coots, comprise the second largest waterbird family. It numbers 127 species worldwide and is represented in southern Africa by 13 breeding species, one summer migrant that visits this region from Europe and one vagrant that occasionally reaches it from North America.

Southern Pochards are classed as 'diving ducks' as they obtain most of their food of plant material and aquatic insects by diving underwater. The male (top) is darker and more richly coloured than the female. Flufftails are notoriously secretive birds, seldom photographed in the wild. Usually their presence is revealed by their ventriloquial hooting calls. Here a male Redchested Flufftail (above), the most common of the southern African flufftails, ventures into a muddy clearing to feed.

The warm buffy colour and crescent-shaped flank feathers of the Fulvous Duck (above)
distinguish it from other ducks though it is similar in habits to the closely related
Whitefaced Duck with which it often associates. One of the most widely distributed of
ducks, it is found throughout Africa and also in Asia and in Central and South America.

Purple Gallinules (above) punctuate their every step with an upward flick of the tail. This exposes the bird's contrasting white undertail coverts and makes it momentarily conspicuous. For the most part vegetarian, these gallinules use their powerful red beaks to break open water lily flowers to get at the seeds and to remove the edible pith from plant stems.

In looking at individual species, one is hard pushed to detect any close relationships: the tiny, secretive, mouselike flufftails that so shun being away from cover seem as far removed from the brazen coot that lives noisily on open water as Cinderella was from her stepsisters. Yet, despite the size differences and the variability in bill and foot shapes, the entire family hangs together anatomically. They all have proportionately long legs and toes (lobed in the coots and other species that swim a lot); short, rounded wings, short tails and narrow bodies designed, it has been suggested, to enable them to squeeze through thick vegetation. All the Rallidae can swim and dive although only coots and a few others spend most of their time in this way. A characteristic of most members of the family is their common habit of nervously flicking their tails up and down. Gallinules and moorhens do so to good effect, showing flashes of their white undertail coverts in the process, but so do the tiny Baillon's Crake and the even smaller flufftails. Although its purpose is not clear, this behaviour is unlikely to have anything at all to do with nervousness. Rather, it may be a means of visual orientation between individuals or it may provide a distraction to a potential predator in pursuit (like the tail-flashing which some antelope species perform in flight). It may even be a trick used by the rail itself to divert the attention of some small creature it is about to eat.

Like other waterbirds, all the species in the family Rallidae move about a great deal in response to the changing availability of their preferred habitats. In most species these movements are nomadic and random, but in at least five cases (involving the African Crake, Striped Crake, Streakybreasted Flufftail, Lesser Moorhen and Lesser Gallinule) the birds undertake a regular southward migration, moving into southern Africa in summer to breed, then moving north again before winter. One species, the Spotted Crake, migrates transcontinentally, leaving its Northern Hemisphere breeding grounds at the end of summer to spend the non-breeding period in Africa.

Resting on one leg, an immature African Jacana (left) displays the enormously long toes that enable it to walk with impunity on floating vegetation. Although this bird is probably too young to fly, its astonishing footgear is already fully developed. Its white underparts, white eyebrow and lack of frontal shield – features only acquired when it is a year old – distinguish it from the adult birds.

Africa's smallest duck, the diminutive
Hottentot Teal (above) is a species that feeds
by dabbling. The sexes can be distinguished by
the colour of their secondaries: the snatch of
metallic green visible in the bird shown here
indicates that it is a male. Shrill whistles pierce
the air as a flock of Whitefaced Ducks (right)
takes to the wing. These birds spend much of
the day loafing on dry ground and feed mostly
after dark, dabbling in shallow water or
swimming with head submerged. Mainly
vegetarian, Whitefaced Ducks eat the seeds
and stems of a variety of aquatic plants.

Most probably do not venture very far south of the equator but in some years they reach southern Africa in numbers. The most remarkable ability to move, however, is demonstrated by the American Purple Gallinule, a North American vagrant. Over the years, no fewer than 23 individuals are known to have survived the rigours of crossing the Atlantic Ocean to reach the western Cape coast. Despite this feat, however, they have not succeeded in establishing a feral population on this side of the Atlantic.

The rails and crakes are, respectively, long-billed and short-billed versions of each other. Most are cryptically marked and secretive in habit and they live close to the water in marshy vegetation. The dapper Black Crake is the exception, being boldly coloured and not reluctant to show itself in the open. Each of the species has its own distinctive voice and were it not for their territorial calling during the breeding season their presence would seldom be detected. This applies even more so to the secretive flufftails which advertise their presence to other conspecifics by uttering mournful hooting notes, their slightly differently pitched or paced call serving to identify the particular species. Most call at dawn or dusk so as to maximize the range and effect of their sound: a flufftail can be heard from a kilometre away in these circumstances. Outside the breeding season their presence is virtually undetectable. One of southern Africa's rarest and least-known birds belongs to this group: this is the Whitewinged Flufftail, the type specimen of which was collected in marshes at Potchefstroom in the western Transvaal in 1876. Since then

The plump body and warm rufous-coloured head and neck identify the Dabchick (below), seen here with its back facing the sun and its tail fluffed out to absorb the warmth of the early morning rays. This small grebe feeds on fish, frogs and aquatic insects which it catches by diving under water. It often follows ducks as they swim, diving below them to catch organisms which they disturb.

five more museum specimens have come from South Africa and 26 have been collected in Ethiopia. The bird has also been recorded at several other localities in South Africa and Zimbabwe but it has never been observed in the wild apart from the brief views it offers in flight after it has been flushed. On these occasions it whirrs away on rounded wings showing distinctive white tips, before dropping out of sight into the vegetation. Nothing is known of its general behaviour: its nest and eggs are undescribed and, until recently, even its call was unknown. It is an altogether mysterious bird whose comings and goings and link, if any, between southern African and Ethiopia, provide a continual source of speculation to ornithologists.

In contrast, most gallinules, moorhens and coots 'let it all hang out': they are conspicuous, bold and brash. The Redknobbed Coot, one of nine species worldwide, is the coot of Africa. It is an abundant waterbird in southern Africa and its population on some waterbodies here can number tens of thousands of birds. It is essentially vegetarian in diet and feeds by dipping under the water to pull up submerged aquatic plants. Sometimes things under the water get it first. A most unfortunate end was the lot of a coot ringed at Barberspan and later recovered in Zululand from the stomach of a crocodile – itself the victim of an unfortunate end when it was run over by a tractor while walking in a sugar-cane field! The Purple Gallinule and Moorhen found in southern Africa both have almost worldwide distributions, but are given various other names in different parts of

The handsome Great Crested Grebe (below) is another diving species that feeds largely on fish. It has a long dagger-like beak similar to that of a kingfisher, and its toes, like those of other grebes, are lobed to enable it to swim under water. This species has an elaborate courtship display during which the crest and ruff (also called ear tippets) are raised and the male and female face each other, wagging their heads from side to side.

their ranges. For example, the gallinule is referred to in places as Purple Swamphen or Purple Coot and the moorhen as Waterhen or Common Gallinule. Both have their 'lesser' counterparts in southern Africa: the Lesser Gallinule and Lesser Moorhen are both erratic migrants that come to southern Africa to breed in years of exceptionally high rainfall. They are more secretive and rail-like than their larger namesakes; skulking in flooded grassland associated with seasonal wetlands, their presence is generally detected by the sound of their distinctive calls emanating from the depths of the marsh.

The Finfoots form another secretive waterbird family which is usually tagged at the end of the Rallidae. Finfoots are cormorant-like in appearance, swimming low in the water and crawling out on to rocks and branches to dry off. The only species found on the continent, appropriately named the African Finfoot, lives in pairs along rivers that have dense fringing vegetation. These birds are reclusive and easily overlooked, retreating into vegetation if disturbed.

Herons, egrets and bitterns which belong to the family Ardeidae (collectively called Ardeids) form another large, cosmopolitan waterbird group. Sixty species occur worldwide, of which 16 breed in southern Africa. A 17th (the Malagassy Squacco Heron) is a rare vagrant and an 18th was a surprise in the form of an American visitor recorded for the first time on the African continent in 1992 when for several months a Little Blue Heron made itself at home on the Berg River estuary in the western Cape. Most Ardeid species occur on more than just one continent and some of those commonly seen in southern Africa, such as the Grey Heron, Purple Heron, Great White Egret, Little Egret and Blackcrowned Night Heron, are also found in Europe, Asia, Australia or even in the Americas.

The largest of Africa's cormorants, seen here in breeding plumage (opposite), is the Whitebreasted Cormorant known as the Great Cormorant in Europe where it occurs in a form which lacks the white breast. The orange mark under the eye and the white spot on the flanks disappear after breeding. It is often hard to credit that ugly ducklings do indeed become swans. Here an elegant-looking Blackcrowned Night Heron parent (above), showing the two white head plumes characteristic of the species, shelters a brood of chicks that only a mother could admire. As its name suggests, this species is nocturnal in its habits and for this reason its eyes are larger than those of other herons.

25

The view a bream or mullet may have seconds before being impaled on the Goliath Heron's deadly beak (above, right). Used as a dagger, the beak is held slightly open so that the victim is speared in two places. The Goliath Heron's great size enables it to prey on larger fish than any other heron and it regularly takes fish with a mass of a half kilogram. Although these birds are capable of killing even larger quarry, sometimes they are unable to swallow them and several are known to have choked to death as a result. Goliath Herons are solitary hunters and wait in ambush at one place for long periods. If unrewarded, they eventually walk quickly to their next station (opposite, above). A close view of the formidable weapon of the world's largest heron (opposite, below).

One species, however, is an endemic breeding bird to the subcontinent. This is the Slaty Egret which has a very restricted breeding range, centring on the Okavango Delta and sometimes extending to adjacent seasonal wetlands in Bushmanland, the Caprivi and Zambia. It is a vagrant to Zimbabwe and even more rare in South Africa. Although the type specimen of this species was collected in the Transvaal in 1895, nearly a century passed before it was seen there again in 1989 when a single bird visited the Nyl floodplain.

It is curious that only three waterbird species are endemic as breeding birds to southern Africa. This level of endemism – about two per cent – is much lower than for birds in the region in general, where the proportion is closer to 15 per cent, and much lower than that found in certain families. For example, more than half of the southern African larks are endemic to the region. The low incidence of endemism in southern African waterbirds is probably best explained by the fact that much of the subcontinent's wetland habitat is ephemeral and waterbirds move about widely to cope with changing conditions. Some are regular migrants, commuting between chosen breeding and non-breeding areas, but the majority are simply nomadic moving as and when circumstances dictate – a wetland that supports 50 000 waterfowl in one year may be a dustbowl in another. Few species dependent on such habitats are able to survive through both wet and dry cycles within a restricted area and consequently few are endemic. Ringing recoveries have shown that the herons, like ducks and rails and other waterbirds, lead nomadic lives, moving from place to place as habitats open up and then close down for them.

The first family thus far considered that feeds primarily on fish is the Ardeidae. It is not alone in this: storks are also fish-eaters, as are grebes, cormorants, pelicans, fish eagles, the Darter and Hamerkop, terns, the African Skimmer and many of the kingfishers.

A Little Egret (left) pauses momentarily while fishing to seek the source of irritation under its wing – possibly a feather louse or mite. The name 'egret' is applied to some smaller heron species, especially those with distinctive breeding plumes known as 'aigrettes'. Delicate and elongated, these were in great demand for hat decoration in the last century. Probably the Little Egret's greatest distinction is its bright yellow toes (above) which, as a result of hormonal changes at the start of breeding, turn red. At the same time the lores (the bare skin between the eyes and the beak) become purplish-red.

Although they are often unrelated, differing in both morphology and technique, most of the fish-eaters have long beaks, either daggers with which they impale their prey, or with hooked tips which enable them to catch and hold firmly on to it. Some species dive underwater to catch fish; some swim along and scoop them up; some fish patiently from perches and others hunt from the wing. Ardeids, like storks, fish on foot. They have long legs which enable them to wade out into fish country, long necks to give them the necessary reach, and they have patience. The basic technique is to walk slowly in shallow water with neck extended and ready to strike. There are variations on this theme and many of the species have subtle tricks and devices to improve their chances of success. A variation involves standing and waiting while occasionally changing position. Common to most of the larger species, this procedure is taken to extremes by the Goliath Heron whose hunting method has been described as a 'jackpot strategy', for instead of catching many little fish to meet their daily needs, these birds rely on taking only two or three large ones. This they do by moving into deep water where they will not be disturbed by other species and waiting, frozen and poised to strike, for long periods. Smaller fish that come into range are ignored while the Goliath Heron waits for the big one, its success depending on keeping still until the right moment. It does, however, have one little trick to relieve the monotony: every now and then it may lean slowly forward and dabble the tip of its beak briefly into the water, apparently to lure fish. This is similar to the technique used in some areas by African fishermen: they lightly whip the water with the tip of their fishing rods for exactly the same purpose.

No two Ardeids fish in identically the same manner. Some species take the non-patient way and deliberately disturb fish by walking about briskly or by running forward, zigzagging, some flicking a wing at intervals to increase the disturbance effect. The Yellowbilled Stork is a great proponent of this technique; Little Egrets, Slaty Egrets and others practise 'foot-stirring', deliberately extending one foot while they are wading and vibrating it on the top of the water for a few seconds. The agitation probably causes small

Saddlebilled Storks are tall, long-legged wading birds whose bold black and white patterned bodies are especially striking when they spread their enormous wings. Although very similar, the sexes can be distinguished by facial characters: the female (right) has a yellow eye and no wattle, while the male (opposite) has a black eye and a yellow wattle hanging below its beak. Found mainly along large rivers, they live in pairs, probably remaining mated for life, and they hunt by catching fish and other small organisms in shallow water.

At rest or in flight, Sacred Ibises, with
their black and white plumage and long,
decurved beaks, are unmistakable. They are
common waterbirds and are highly gregarious,
often found among other species (right) if not
in groups of their own. The necks and heads of
immature birds (below) are feathered whereas
in adults this area is covered by black skin.
Sacred Ibises have a varied diet, ranging from
offal and carrion to beetles, frogs, fish and eggs
of other birds. Nesting occurs colonially and
several pairs may breed on a single large
platform. From the outset, nestlings have black
heads (above), and from the age of two to three
weeks they wander about the colony in groups.

fish to move and so become visible to the egret. While hunting in shallow water, herons often tilt their heads and necks to one side. Close examination will reveal that they invariably incline them in the direction of the sun, apparently in an effort to reduce the glare on the targeted area of water ahead of them. It is not clear how they have learnt to accommodate for parallax error when making a strike: water bends light making the fish appear further away than it really is. For the jackpot hunters, much more is lost than the fish by a missed strike: the site has been disturbed, the time spent settling in there, wasted. Probably for this reason herons usually fly off to start in a new place after making an unsuccessful strike.

Because of their greater visibility, the large herons steal most of the family's limelight. Yet most of the southern African Ardeids (for example, the Squacco, Greenbacked and Rufousbellied Herons) are relatively small birds. Some are secretive, and the nocturnal Whitebacked Night Heron and three bittern species are seldom seen at all. They feed on fish but generally have a more diversified diet as they also prey on frogs and tadpoles, crabs and aquatic insects.

Other fish-hunting waterbird families represented in southern Africa include grebes, of which there are three resident species in the region (Great Crested Grebe, Blacknecked Grebe and Dabchick), cormorants, with two freshwater species and three marine species (not discussed here), and the Darter. Although unrelated, these species hunt fish underwater by diving below the surface and swimming after their prey. Marine cormorants plunge to depths of nearly 100 metres (penguins can descend to depths of 240 metres) but the two mainly inland species, the Whitebreasted Cormorant and Reed Cormorant, do not dive deeper than six metres, perhaps because there is no necessity to do so. Darters fish at shallower depths, diving only one to four metres below the surface. All the underwater fishers have large webbed or lobed feet set well back on their bodies and make short dives, lasting less than a minute. Another means of decreasing buoyancy and improving the ability to dive – so it has been suggested – is stone swallowing, a recorded habit of a race of the Whitebreasted Cormorant. These birds, and particularly the Darter, have a more wettable plumage than other swimming waterbirds such as ducks, and this is another adaptation construed as reducing their buoyancy and helping them to dive. These birds often hang their wings open after swimming, a characteristic that has been linked to the greater wettability of their plumage and to the perceived need to dry it.

Pelicans, another very distinctive family of fish-hunting waterbirds, are represented by two species in southern Africa (and seven worldwide). They are large, heavy birds whose enormous wingspan enables them to soar and to cover great distances. Even during the breeding cycle when pairs are confined to nests, those off-duty commute daily between the breeding colony and fishing sites up to 100 kilometres away. Southern Africa's two pelicans often loaf side by side on the shores of lakes but they do not share fishing time. The smaller Pinkbacked Pelican fishes solitarily, usually close inshore, using its large bill to scoop up its prey. The larger White Pelican is more sociable and forages co-operatively, the birds forming lines which drive fish shoals into shallow water where they are surrounded by the group and caught.

A great deal has been written about the relative hunting performances of the two large diurnal birds of prey that live by fishing. One, the African Fish Eagle, is among the best known of Africa's large birds. It hunts solitarily, usually watching the water from a perch and making a shallow dive at prey when it is sighted. It preys mostly on fish about half a kilogram in weight which it snatches out of the water with one foot and then takes to

A brush of stiff, bristle-like feathers on the back of the head gives the Crowned Crane (opposite) its name and makes its appearance quite different from that of other crane species. The bright red gular sac at its throat is inflated when the bird utters its deep, booming call. This call, rendered as 'mahem' (the bird's Afrikaans name), is a familiar sound in southern Africa's larger upland marshes.

Seldom seen in such an exposed position, an African Rail (above) moves cautiously from one reedbed to another. Most rails, including this species, are extremely secretive and it is only their calls that give away their presence. This species utters a rapid series of whistled notes which it can often be induced to produce by clapping hands at the edge of the reeds.

a perch to eat. In East Africa it has been reckoned that fish eagles have an easy life, hunting, on average, for a mere eight minutes a day. They also pirate food from other more diligent fishers including pelicans, herons and the Osprey which often share the same fishing waters. Ospreys are smaller than fish eagles and take smaller fish – 200 grams on average. They hunt from perches as fish eagles do but have the added advantage of being proficient at hovering, often hunting from the wing in the absence of perches. A third fish-eating bird of prey in the region is the elusive Pel's Fishing Owl. Entirely nocturnal, it hunts in the dark from vantage points above pools along slow-moving rivers. Unfortunately, many rivers of this kind in the eastern parts of southern Africa have deteriorated to the extent that these owls are disappearing from the region and their stronghold remains the Okavango Delta. The gulls and terns form a large, mostly piscivorous family known as the Laridae that are characteristically birds of the sea. If skimmers and skuas are included in this group (as they sometimes are, though not here) there are 96 species worldwide. Most of the southern African species are marine, but two (the Greyheaded Gull and Caspian Tern) live both inland and along the coast, and two (the Whiskered Tern and African Skimmer) are entirely restricted to freshwater habitats. In addition to being favoured by these four breeding species, southern African wetlands are visited in summer by Whitewinged Terns, which are common migrants from the Palearctic, and

from time to time by other Northern Hemisphere gulls (such as Franklin's Gull from North America) and terns (such as the Gullbilled Tern from the Mediterranean), all of which are rare vagrants.

The kingfisher's image as a fish-eating waterbird is to some extent a false one since more than half the 86 species found worldwide lead terrestrial lives and feed on insects. Only four of southern Africa's 10 species are aquatic (Giant Kingfisher, Pied, Half-collared and Malachite). They feed on fish to a greater or lesser extent and also catch crabs (a favourite prey of the Giant Kingfisher), tadpoles and aquatic insects.

Many animals, from whales to ducks, feed by sieving and thus trapping food particles in the water by passing it through filters in their mouths. Flamingos, those delicate, long-legged, long-necked, pink birds that add elegance to every wetland they grace, are among this élite clan and their beaks are actually highly evolved, extraordinary-looking food filters. Thick and banana-shaped, they curve downwards in the middle so that when they are opened the gap is of equal width along its length. The inner rim is fringed with lamellae which sieve the water as it enters and leaves, while the tongue, in moving forward and back, pumps water into and out of the chamber. Two of the world's five flamingo species occur in southern Africa, often living alongside one another and, at first sight, appearing to lead very similar lives. A closer look, however, reveals that the feeding

The diminutive Little Bittern (above) is usually only noticed once it has been disturbed and taken to flight, thus revealing a bold cream and black upperwing pattern. The birds often avoid detection in vegetation by adopting a 'bittern posture': they point their beaks upward and draw in their bodies to appear as thin as possible.

37

Droplets fly as a Blacksmith Plover takes a bath (above). A session of preening, in which the damp feathers are carefully groomed with the beak, invariably follows such bathing, a procedure which serves to maintain the plumage in good condition. Blacksmith Plovers are common shorebirds found almost wherever land meets water.

behaviour of the two species is quite different even though both forage by inverting their beaks in water which they pump through the filter. The larger species (the Greater Flamingo) has a shallow-keeled upper mandible with coarse filters while the smaller (the Lesser Flamingo) has a deep-keeled beak equipped with finer filters. Lesser Flamingos are 'top feeders', seeking food only in the few centimetres closest to the surface of the water while constantly moving, either by swimming or wading, and sweeping their large beaks like scythes across the water. In contrast, the Greater Flamingo is a 'bottom feeder' and often submerges its whole head while foraging. It tends to remain in one place, stamping its feet and rotating slowly until it completes a full circle before moving on. Its foot movements stir food particles into suspension so that they can be trapped when filtered through its beak. The coarser filters in its beak enable the Greater Flamingo to take larger – mainly animal – food items such as crustaceans, molluscs, shrimps and fly larvae measuring one to six millimetres. The filters of the Lesser Flamingo prevent larger particles from entering the beak, those that are trapped being from about one millimetre in size down to about 0,01 millimetres. These birds are mainly vegetarian and feed mostly on algae and diatoms, vast quantities of which are produced in some tropical alkaline lakes and pans where flamingo numbers can reach thousands – and indeed millions – in extreme conditions.

The last large waterbird group consists of those collectively known as waders or shorebirds (the latter name is preferable as the term 'wader' covers storks and herons which also wade) and includes a number of different families. The most numerous is the family Scolopacidae (the so-called scolopacids – sandpipers, stints, snipe, godwits, phalaropes), of which 35 species have been recorded in southern Africa. With only one exception (the Ethiopian Snipe), these shorebirds are all non-resident, migrating here from their breeding grounds in the Northern Hemisphere to spend the northern winter (but austral summer) on our lagoons and estuaries, sometimes in flocks numbering thousands of birds. Thirty years ago fewer than 20 scolopacid species had been recorded in southern Africa but the list has steadily increased as birdwatchers have sharpened their identification skills and newer and better field guides have become available. The most recent addition to the list of scolopacids, a 'first' for both southern Africa and the African continent as a whole, was a Hudsonian Godwit recorded at Port Elizabeth in 1987. Scores of birdwatchers flocked to the Zwartkops Estuary to see this unusual American vagrant and the following year it, and a second bird at Langebaan, were seen again. Next year it may be a Canadian Spotted Sandpiper that has somehow mixed up its continents to reach southern African waters, or perhaps an Eskimo Curlew...

Unravelling the identity of rare scolopacids and ticking off a new one for southern Africa provides a reason to live for many fanatical birders, but the family also provides much interest for lesser mortals. Their migration is spectacular. Each year literally millions of shorebirds which breed in the Arctic fly south, some travelling 13 000 kilometres to spend their non-breeding period in Africa's wetlands – as a large number of recoveries of ringed birds has proved. In fact a Ruff, ringed in the eastern Cape and recovered in the Kolyma Basin in eastern Siberia, is the most distant recovery yet obtained of any ringed land bird. The logistics of this twice-a-year marathon are intriguing. The flight is fuelled by fat and in the weeks prior to migrating the birds increase their mass by 50 to 60 per cent by accumulating fat. A Curlew Sandpiper, for example, with a lean mass of 53 grams, leaves weighing 80 grams; a smaller Little Stint increases its mass from 21 grams to 33 grams while a Greenshank increases its weight from about 160 grams to about 290 grams.

The slim, dapper Marsh Sandpiper feeds by walking about briskly in shallow water and pecking at small insects at the surface (top). It is usually found on its own; when flushed it takes off uttering a sharp 'teuk' note and then looks much like a small version of a Greenshank. Cape Wagtails (above) also frequent the bare shores of open pans and dams, a habitat very different from the suburban gardens to which they have adapted so successfully.

A Blackwinged Stilt baths, first submerging and absorbing water into the feathers (above), then giving a vigorous flap to shake off the excess drops (right). This species, which is quite unmistakable with its black and white plumage and long red legs, forages by wading, usually knee-deep, and picking small items off the surface of the water. Often seen in groups, Blackwinged Stilts are noisy birds, uttering a shrill 'kik' to maintain contact or repeating the note more shrilly when agitated.

The Blackwinged Stilt is found on five continents and has a range as wide as that of any shorebird.

Visually, there is little to distinguish the Cape Reed Warbler (above) from a host of other 'little brown jobs' that live alongside it in marshland habitats. When it sings, however, the bird is immediately identifiable by the melodious warbling it produces. Its evocative song is one of the characteristic sounds of the reedbed, and one which enriches the ambience of the wetlands.

The fast-flying Greenshanks probably cross Africa in one leg, making the 7 500 kilometre trip from the south to the Mediterranean by flying continuously at 80 kilometres an hour for four days and nights. Their fat load provides fuel for a flight of about 7 700 kilometres. Smaller waders have a shorter range and require two or three stop-overs to refuel *en route*. Many southern African-ringed birds have been re-trapped on the East African Rift Valley lakes (Lake Nakuru, Lake Magadi and others), indicating that these wetlands are a vital link in their migration, and the Caspian and Black seas are other probable transit lounges for birds flying to the Taimyar Peninsula to breed. Sanderlings, which live on the southern African coast, probably take a different route up the west coast, using the Gulf of Guinea as a stop-over, then continuing to the Mediterranean, North or Caspian Sea before making the final leg to their breeding grounds. In each case the migration is accomplished by accumulating fat, flying a leg to a known transit site, refuelling and flying a second leg, and so on. The journey lasts between six and seven weeks, one of which is spent flying and the remainder on feeding *en route*.

A second interesting feature of shorebirds' life is the way in which their breeding success in the Arctic is linked to lemming cycles and the manner in which this is manifested in the populations that spend their non-breeding season in southern Africa. It has been best demonstrated in the Curlew Sandpiper which is one of the most abundant scolopacids to reach the subcontinent, but the phenomenon occurs equally in Knots, Little Stints, Turnstones and others. Lemmings undergo a population explosion every three years and when this occurs they provide a rich food source for predators, principally Arctic foxes, living in the Arctic tundra. During these periods, when the foxes are eating the abundant lemmings instead of chicks and eggs, the waders nesting in the tundra escape the high predation rates they would otherwise suffer and produce many more young. This is reflected at the other end of the world where the birds spend winter: after

Confiding and ever curious, a Cape Reed Warbler (left) ventures cautiously to the edge of its haven in the bulrushes to view the passing scene. During the summer breeding season, Cape Reed Warblers build neat cup-shaped nests which they suspend between two plant stems. Pairs are territorial at this time and the entire reedbed is staked out into their separate domains.

43

'lemming years' the proportion of juveniles in these populations is high (up to 30 per cent), whereas after 'non-lemming years' it is low (below 10 per cent). Thus, at Lange-baan Lagoon Curlew Sandpipers had numerous young in the summers of 1982-3, 1985-6 and 1988-9, each of which followed a 'lemming year' in the Arctic, and they had proportionately fewer young in the intervening years.

Plovers are another large shorebird family although many of the species are not waterbirds. Eight of those tied to wetlands breed in southern Africa and a further six are non-breeding visitors or vagrants from other continents. Some, like the Blacksmith Plover, are common, well-known birds present on virtually every waterbody on the subcontinent, while others, like the Whitecrowned and Chestnutbanded Plovers, have very restricted habitats or ranges. Plovers differ from scolopacids by finding their prey visually; sandpipers and stints, on the other hand, are mostly tactile feeders. When feeding in mud, some of the plovers use a technique not unlike that used by the Little Egret in the water: they extend one foot forward and tremble it lightly on the mud, presumably to lure prey to the surface.

One or two waterbirds occur among the other shorebird families. Dikkops are plover-like birds that have large yellow eyes to accommodate their nocturnal habits. One species, the Water Dikkop, is dependent on aquatic habitats. Another plover-like family, but having truncated legs, is the pratincoles of which two of the southern African species are aquatic. They have long, thin wings, feed aerially and have a tern-like flight, wheeling and swooping about in flocks. Lastly, the Jacana and Painted Snipe are two closely allied waterbird families that are of special interest because of their unusual breeding behaviour. Parental roles are reversed and females are polyandrous, mating with a succession of males each of which looks after the clutch laid for it.

Swallows, warblers and wagtails are three large passerine families which have among their numbers a few species that depend on aquatic habitats. The warblers, in particular, include a group living in sedge and reed marshes (appropriately called Sedge, Reed or Marsh Warblers) and are wholly restricted to such aquatic habitats. These are small, brown-coloured insectivorous birds that hop about among the stems of marsh vegetation. They all have loud, distinctive songs – melodious in some species, but harsh and grating in others – which are often the only indication of the bird's presence. Many are migratory, some coming to winter in southern Africa from the Northern Hemisphere where they breed; others migrating from central Africa to nest in the wetlands in the south. None of them is endemic to the subcontinent. These, and other waterbirds will be reappearing in different guises in the pages that follow.

The dramatic transformation from non-breeding (opposite, above) to breeding plumage (opposite, below) in the Whitewinged Tern occurs shortly before these trans-continental migrants leave southern Africa for their breeding grounds in the Northern Hemisphere. These birds are common in their winter quarters, gracing many an open body of water with their gentle presence. In their winter plumage they appear similar to the Whiskered Tern, another species found on inland waters and with which they often share air space.

WEB OF WATER
WHERE WATERBIRDS LIVE

*Avocets (left) are close kin of the Blackwinged Stilt
and the two are often found together. Like stilts, Avocets
are gregarious and forage by wading about knee-deep,
sweeping their unusually-shaped beaks from side to side
through the water in a scything motion. In deeper
water Avocets are not reluctant to swim, and continue
to feed by sweeping the beak back and forth in the
same rhythmic manner.*

SOUTHERN AFRICA IS A SEMI-ARID subcontinent; richly endowed in so many other natural resources, it was not dealt a good hand in rainfall. The subcontinent's overall annual mean (about 450 millimetres) is only about half the world's average for it straddles the Southern Hemisphere's drought-belt latitudes in which the prevailing high pressure systems are not conducive to the formation of rain. Not only is the average annual rainfall low but it is inconsistent. In fact, the term 'average' has little meaning since, in the drier regions, an 'average' amount of rain rarely falls in a given year: it is a matter of drought or flood, famine or feast. Consequently many of the region's west-flowing rivers remain dry for most of the time, only running intermittently during the boom years, and the natural wetlands across much of the subcontinent are dry as often as they are wet.

Most people living in cities are cushioned from the reality of climatic vicissitudes. Generally, droughts mean that they are restricted to watering their gardens twice a week while floods indicate that they need to take umbrellas to work. City-dwellers are largely ignorant of the sophisticated planning and feats of engineering that ensure that they have water and power, nor are they aware of the enormous impact these developments have on the natural functioning of rivers and wetlands. Not so the waterbirds which respond swiftly and positively to the rise and fall of wetland habitats, some created randomly and unpredictably by chance events taking place in the atmosphere, others by the hand of man. Waterbirds not seen within hundreds of kilometres of pans in the Kalahari arrive to nest there when these fill with water; newly built dams that stop the flow of a river for long distances downstream but create nutrient-filled shallows in their upper-reaches draw in waterbirds like a magnet. A year later the water, and the waterbirds, may have vanished from these places.

Rivers are the threads that link many of the subcontinent's wetlands. In most cases they are also their sole source of water. Rivers feed the network of coastal lakes, lagoons and estuaries that are scattered along the eastern seaboard of Mozambique and Zululand and extend southwards through the Cape to the west coast. They carry an enormous volume of water out of Angola's highlands and discharge it into the Okavango Delta or into the floodplains of the Caprivi. They provide the water that from time to time inundates the Etosha and Makgadikgadi pans and transforms these hostile landscapes into suitable breeding habitats for flamingos and pelicans. Rivers are the veins and blood of wetlands although, according to some definitions, they themselves are not wetlands.

What is a wetland? The Okavango, with its clear water, stretches of blue water lilies, rafts of papyrus and ubiquitous fish eagles, is an image that immediately springs to mind. It is indeed a wetland but only one of many kinds. Because of the great variety of wetlands and the conflicting perspectives of different people with an interest in them (conservationists, ecologists, agriculturalists, hydrologists and others), it is as difficult to settle on a definition that caters for everyone as it is to define a waterbird. Some definitions of wetlands specifically exclude openwater habitats – lakes, pans, rivers – while others are so all-embracing that they virtually include the sea. Here are some examples:

'Wetlands are areas with waterlogged soils dominated by emergent vegetation.' (Davies and Day)

'Wetlands are those areas that are inundated or saturated by surface or ground water at a frequency and duration sufficient to support, and that under normal circumstances do support, a prevalence of vegetation typically adapted for life in saturated water conditions.' (Natal Wetland Research Programme, based on USA definition.)

Standing on one leg and with the calm water as a mirror, an Avocet grooms its feathers (opposite). Feather maintenance is an important daily activity in the lives of waterbirds and the heavy-billed Caspian Tern (above) is seen here stretching its wings in similar comfort behaviour. Many of the postures adopted by birds become ritualized in other forms of behaviour: preening, for example, may be a displacement activity observed in birds torn between fleeing or attacking.

*With good reason, and unredeemed by their bright colours, Purple Gallinules
(above) have been called the thugs of the marshland bird community. They rob the nests
of other birds of their eggs and chicks; they litter the area with the chewed remains
of plants that they eat and they utter the most discordant noises imaginable.*

'Wetlands are areas of marsh, fen, peatland or water whether natural or artificial, permanent or temporary, with water that is static or flowing, fresh, brackish or salt, including areas of marine waters, the depth of which at low tide does not exceed six metres.' (Ramsar Convention)

'A wetland is land where an excess of water is the dominant factor determining the nature of soil development and the types of animal and plant communities living at the soil surface. It spans a continuum of environments where terrestrial and aquatic systems intergrade.' (US Fish & Wildlife Service)

Alice in Wonderland would have solved two dilemmas simultaneously, albeit in a circular way, by defining a wetland as a place used by waterbirds and a waterbird as a bird that uses a wetland. Wetlands, and their attendant rivers, have come and gone over geological time. The web of fossil watercourses covering the southern Kalahari owes its presence to a wetter era in the subcontinent's history. The Makgadikgadi Pan complex, which today sees water only intermittently and in favourable sections, was in the past a great inland lake into which the upper section of the Zambezi River discharged. Langebaan Lagoon, which is today an enclosed arm of the sea, originated as the estuary of the Berg River before the river changed course, so starving the lagoon of fresh water.

Similarly, the lakes that dot the southern and eastern coastal plains of the subcontinent were once estuaries where rivers met the sea. As the coastline extended seaward they became progressively more landlocked and divergent in character. The array of wetlands we see today on the subcontinent is but a momentary freeze in the kaleidoscope of ever-changing landscapes that mark the passage of time and the rhythm of wet and dry cycles over the millennia. A glimpse into the past (or future) was offered in the early 1970s when most of southern Africa experienced exceptionally high rainfall – in some places about twice the annual mean. Wetlands were created across the subcontinent; flamingos bred on pans in the northern Cape; massive mixed breeding colonies of herons and egrets were established at such divergent sites as Barberspan, the Nata mouth (into Sua Pan) and the Nyl floodplain, and many waterbirds previously rare or unknown as breeders in the region nested here. Within a decade the pendulum had swung back and drought once more prevailed across southern Africa.

The different types of wetlands found in southern African are not unique to the subcontinent but can be categorized according to the system developed to classify wetlands in other parts of the world. At its broadest, five systems are recognized: marine, estuarine, riverine, lacustrine (lakes) and palustrine (marshes). Each of these in turn is divisible into two or more subsystems: lakes, for example, have edges (littoral) and deepwater (limnetic) subsystems which in turn have a range of substrata. Each system or subsystem is modified by the prevailing water regime (for example, whether it is permanent, seasonal or intermittently flooded), by the water chemistry (for example, whether it is freshwater or saline) and by the presence and nature of aquatic vegetation. These expand the classification to 'class level' – for example, to a seasonally flooded saline marsh or a permanent freshwater lake.

In most cases the choice of habitat made by waterbirds overlaps these system boundaries. A few species are likely to be found on any and every aquatic habitat, be it riverine, lacustrine or palustrine; whether it is intermittently or permanently flooded, saline or freshwater. The majority, however, exhibit greater constraint. Caspian Terns and Redknobbed Coots choose openwater habitats; the tern using lacustrine, estuarine and marine waters, whereas the coot is confined to non-saline lacustrine waters.

The Redknobbed Coot (below) is one of the most conspicuous, common and widespread of southern Africa's waterbirds. Its black plumage renders it unmistakable and its vegetarian diet enables it to feel at home on virtually any waterbody. Some dams support hundreds or even thousands of these highly gregarious, inoffensive weed-eaters.

The splendid African Fish Eagle, one of the few birds of prey to be dependent on wetlands, lives on fish which it catches in its talons after a swift dive (right). It also scavenges, eating dead fish and other creatures that are washed up on the shore (above). Pairs of African Fish Eagles often feed together; they live year-round in territories which they proclaim with their loud yelping calls, often uttered in duet, the male's note being higher pitched than that of the female.

Vegetated habitats are favoured by most Rallidae; some, like the Purple Gallinule, have a wide tolerance, others, like the Lesser Gallinule, are more restricted in their choice of habitat. They, for example, are confined to seasonally flooded freshwater wetlands with emergent vegetation.

Water salinity or brackishness is a consideration in some species such as the Cape Teal and Avocet. In others, the size of the wetland is of concern: pelicans, for example, are mainly confined to large waterbodies. Overall, most waterbirds select for class (or lower order) distinctions rather than for system (higher order) distinctions in their choice of wetland habitats: for instance, for the fish-eaters it matters nothing if the water in which they fish is estuarine, lacustrine or riverine as long as it is shallow, has good visibility and supports fish populations.

If the generic compartments of this wetland classification do not reflect the habitat preferences of waterbirds, what does? First, the type of food eaten by each species sets constraints on where that bird is likely to be successful. Secondly, the way it forages and the tools at its disposal for foraging (leg-length, bill-shape, and so on) further limit it. Thirdly, in order to nest successfully many waterbird species require not just a food source and a mate but a particular situation or type of cover where their eggs and young can remain undetected by, or their nests are inaccessible to, predators. Thus, a jacana that wanders into the Namib Desert may survive at a waterhole but it could not successfully nest in such a situation if it lacked the floating plants that provide nest cover. Similarly, the flocks of thousands of flamingos that adorn many seasonal pans in southern Africa would long ago have become extinct were it not for the safety of Etosha or Makgadik-gadi to which they retreat for breeding. The nesting habitat chosen by some species bears no resemblance to their feeding habitat. For example, many herons which forage by wading in open water and would be classed as openwater species, retreat to the safety of dense reedbeds to nest.

If the specialized breeding habitats of some species are excluded, the majority of waterbirds prefer either open water or open shores, or they choose aquatic habitats offering some concealment in the form of emergent vegetation. A few others are specifically restricted to flowing water (rivers). Openwater habitats, wetlands with emergent vegetation and rivers are sometimes inextricably mixed; floodplains often form such mosaics and species with quite different habitat preferences then occur alongside one another, blurring any distinctions that may be seen in other situations. The following chapters take a closer look at these three habitats and the birds that are characteristically associated with each.

The Cape Teal (opposite), which frequents temporary, brackish waters, is more tolerant of high water salinity than other southern African ducks. A typical 'dabbling duck', it feeds with head and neck submerged. At rest, the Redwinged Pratincole (above, right) presents an image quite different from that seen while it is in flight. Hidden from view are its long, pointed wings and deeply forked tail, features which transform it into a graceful, swallow-like aerial hunter on the wing.

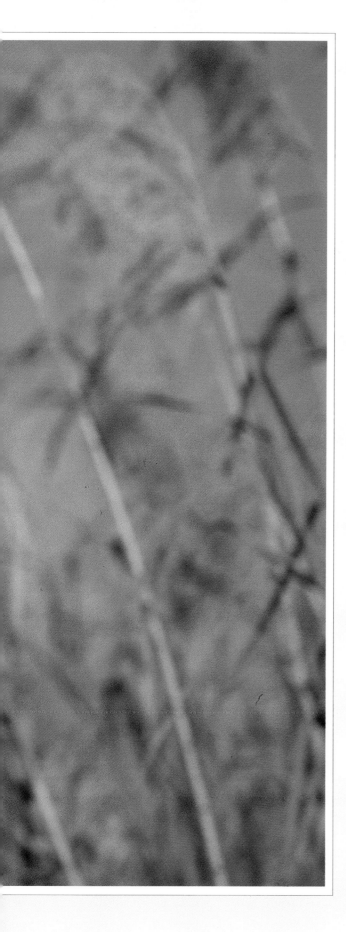

REQUIEM

FOR RIVERS

A long-winged African Skimmer flies purposefully along a reed-lined channel of the Okavango River. These river specialists are regular visitors to southern Africa's northern areas, arriving at the end of summer after water levels have peaked. They stay to breed on sandbars exposed in the rivers during the low flow, and leave again as the water rises.

REQUIEM
FOR RIVERS

RIVERS ARE RESPONSIBLE FOR the most spectacular of geological processes: they whittle away mountains, transport millions of tons of sediment out to the oceans each year and have created some of southern Africa's most interesting scenery – natural wonders such as the Fish River Canyon, the Blyde River Canyon and the gorge below the great Augrabies Falls. They cover the landscape like the veins on a hand – little streams coalescing, becoming larger, weaving and meandering, until, in bloated maturity, they arrive at the sea. They are the thread that links and provisions a diversity of wetlands along the way, from the upland sponges at the heads of catchments to their lower reaches where they may fan out into floodplains or widen into estuaries, or simply discharge through an open mouth into the sea.

The essential ecological character of a river is its flow. Rivers are termed lotic – that is, flowing – ecosystems to distinguish them from non-flowing – lentic – ecosystems. Their characteristics and their faunal and floral communities change progressively downstream as the gradient, the volume of flow, the nature of the underlying rock and other things, change. In their infancy, when they set out as mountain streams, they have a low productivity, are fast-flowing, rich in oxygen and low in dissolved salts. They have a limited insect and fish fauna which is adapted to survive in such conditions – insects with grapples and suckers enabling them to 'stay put' in the fast stream, and predominantly small-bodied fish. Plankton, unable to resist the stream flow, is absent, and so are plankton-feeding birds like flamingos and shovellers. As these streams join and widen and attain shallower gradients, rivers enter their middle reaches and their character changes. The water is less turbulent, so less free oxygen is present; it carries more sediment and is thus more turbid, and muddy bottoms and sheltered banks expand the niches available to a more varied and richer insect and fish community. This pattern continues into the river's lower reaches until it meets the coast.

Some may discharge into the sea through an open mouth but most southern African rivers terminate in estuaries which are coastal lakes that open intermittently or continuously to the sea. The salinity of the sea and its tidal action have a major effect on the nature of the estuary and its biotic community. Nutrient-rich mud flats are successively exposed and covered by tidal action and provide an important habitat for shorebirds which use some estuaries in vast numbers. The protected waters provide nursery areas to shoals of pelagic fish and these in turn attract a variety of piscivorous birds. The salinity of estuaries varies depending on the flow of fresh water into the system which, in turn, is determined by the time of year and by droughts and floods, and faunal communities fluctuate in response to the saline-freshwater mix. Lake St Lucia (in Zululand), Africa's largest coastal lake, has seen large annual fluctuations in its salinity level as a result of variable river flow and consequently there have been profound changes to its avifauna. Periods of high salinity attract flamingos in their thousands; when the tide swings to low salinity they move away and the ducks and coots move in.

This succession is, or was, typical of the subcontinent's rivers, but in recent times things have changed dramatically. Rivers in southern Africa provide virtually all the water used for human consumption in its myriad of ways: for growing crops, for domestic use, for industry, for generating power or for mining. Water is measured in cubic metres (one cubic metre equals 1 000 litres); the average annual runoff from all South Africa's rivers combined is estimated to be 53 500 million cubic metres. More than half a million dams, with a combined capacity of over half the total annual runoff, have been built to trap and store this water and their effect on rivers is enormous. From the dams,

Still wet from its last dive, a male Pied Kingfisher (opposite) alertly watches
the water below. In this species the sexes are distinguished by the breast markings:
males have two bands, females only one. The huge Giant Kingfisher (above)
also exhibits sexual dimorphism in its front markings. Here a female is recognized by
its chestnut belly and black breast; in males these colours are reversed. In the absence
of perches, both species may fish by hovering over water.

*Only when it clambers on to a rock to dry off does the African Finfoot (above)
display its most colourful asset – its feet. Even young birds scarcely out of the nest
have the waxy red legs of the adult. Here a female, duller plumaged than the male,
rests between spells of foraging along the sheltered edges of a river.*

water is abstracted at a current rate of about 20 million cubic metres per annum and the two-fold effect of this storage and abstraction is that river flow has been greatly decreased. In drought years the dams have the capacity to trap practically all runoff and many once-perennial rivers simply run dry. The rivers of the Kruger National Park are an example: once perennial, most now cease flowing in winter as a result of water storage and abstraction upstream. The decline in 80 per cent of South Africa's threatened fish species is attributed to the loss of water flow.

Loss of water is but one of a long list of problems besetting southern Africa's rivers. Large dams have the added impact of flooding riverine habitat: the two huge lakes built along the Zambezi, Kariba and Cahora Bassa have, between them, drowned more than 500 kilometres of this great river. Furthermore, they trap the silt that floods formerly carried downstream and created sandbars. When water is released from Lake Kariba, a metre-high tidal wave rushes downstream, sweeping away the nests of any birds using the low islands. Unfortunately for the aquatic fauna downstream from these and other large dams, the water-releases are not always advantageously timed. South Africa's largest dam, the Hendrik Verwoerd, situated on the Orange River, discharges more water in winter (when the demand for electricity is highest) than in summer and the resulting surges of water may trigger the fish to spawn at the least favourable time of the year (when temperatures are at their lowest).

Equally serious for aquatic life is the deterioration in water quality as a consequence of runoff of one sort or another into the rivers. Invariably, a proportion of the fertilizers applied to lands to grow crops finds its way into rivers and dams and so stimulates the growth of unwanted algal mats or of floating rafts of aquatic plants. Water Hyacinth, Kariba Weed, Water Fern and others are aliens that have become a serious problem in many waters enriched in this way. Rivers that drain out of coal-mined landscapes are beset with the particular problem of acidification resulting from their taking up sulphur from the coal tailings, while from time to time toxic effluent discharged by factories into rivers also leads to the mass mortality of fish. It is no exaggeration to say that there is not a single pristine river catchment left in southern Africa and that many once biologically rich river courses on the subcontinent have been so degraded that they have become little more than drains transporting man's waste and toxic effluent away to the sea.

How have the waterbirds coped in the face of this onslaught on the rivers? Relatively few of southern Africa's birds are strictly confined to rivers: only seven species are entirely restricted to this habitat; another seven occur mainly along rivers and about 15 more occur commonly on them. Of the first seven, three species occur widely: African Black Duck (sometimes referred to as Black River Duck in recognition of its habitat preference), Halfcollared Kingfisher, and Longtailed Wagtail. The fourth species is the shy, elusive African Finfoot which is less widely distributed while the last three are birds of large, tropical African rivers that are on the southern fringe of their range in the subcontinent. The rarest of these is the little Rock Pratincole that never ventures south of the Zambezi, Chobe and Kavango rivers; then the African Skimmer which seldom does while the Whitecrowned Plover is found along the sandy stretches of larger east-flowing rivers as far as the southern end of the Kruger National Park.

Rock Pratincoles and African Skimmers would appear to have been impacted in two ways by the developments along the Zambezi River. First, they have lost hundreds of kilometres of former breeding habitat as a result of the construction of the two huge dams and, secondly, unseasonal water-releases from Lake Kariba take their toll on nesting

The drab-coloured African Black Duck (above) lives in pairs along rivers. It favours streams with stony bottoms, particularly those with sufficient protruding rocks to provide it with places to bask and preen. Like other 'dabbling ducks', it feeds by submerging its bill or by 'upending' in deeper water. Its varied diet includes a range of plant material and aquatic insects.

colonies. Both species nest colonially close to the water level during the spring low flow period, the pratincoles on exposed rocks and the skimmers on exposed sandbars. It is curious that African Skimmers nested at the mouth of Lake St Lucia in Zululand, way out of their normal range, for two successive years in the early 1940s though this has not been repeated in the half-century since then. However, in 1983 and 1984 a few pairs attempted to breed on the Runde River in south-eastern Zimbabwe and from time to time single vagrant birds are seen in the most unlikely places across South Africa.

Whitecrowned Plovers liven up the rivers they frequent with their shrill piping calls and their constant flying back and forth, made all the more conspicuous by their stark white wings. Like skimmers, they nest on sandbars in early summer when the risk of flooding is minimal. Their eggs, also laid on exposed sandbars, are subject to searing temperatures and were it not for their habit of wetting their belly feathers and cooling their eggs (and chicks) with water in this way, their hatching success would be much lower. Skimmers behave in the same way, as do the Rock Pratincoles and some of the other plover species. While pratincoles and skimmers have declined, the Whitecrowned Plover has increased its southward range in the past decade. In the 1970s it occurred only as far south as the northernmost rivers in the Kruger National Park but in the 1980s it has moved towards its current southern limit on the Crocodile River. Reduced water flow in the eastern Transvaal lowveld may actually have benefited this species by providing it with greater expanses of its preferred sandy habitat.

Skimmers and pratincoles are seasonal visitors to their breeding areas, arriving in about May when the water levels are receding and departing when they rise again in

Three characteristic river-loving species: the African Pied Wagtail (below, left), the Longtailed Wagtail (below, right) and the Common Sandpiper (opposite). The two wagtail species are river-residents, living in pairs in well-demarcated territories where singing (below, left) is one way in which they proclaim their occupancy. Unlike the Cape Wagtail, neither of these species has adapted itself to the suburban garden environment in southern Africa. Instead, they live like diminutive sandpipers along the shores and shallows of rivers and streams, tails bobbing up and down as they trip about the rocks and sandbanks in search of small insects and larvae.

In the light of the late afternoon sun, a wide-eyed Water Dikkop is caught bathing (above). During the day, these cryptically coloured nocturnal birds lie up among flood debris and bushes on beaches and the edges of rivers. At night they come alive, proclaiming their presence by uttering bursts of penetrating whistles.

mid-summer. To some extent the Whitecrowned Plover is also displaced from rivers it nests on in summer when the water rises. By contrast, the three commonest river birds, African Black Duck, Halfcollared Kingfisher and Longtailed Wagtail, stay year-round in one place. They live in pairs, most remaining mated for life, and are territorial, excluding conspecifics from their chosen stretches of river. Along the Eerste River in the south-western Cape where the Black Duck has been intensively studied, pairs defend, on average, about 700 metres of river; Longtailed Wagtails, which have been the subject of a second study on the Palmiet River in Durban, hold territories averaging about 600 metres in length. In these threads of space the ducks and wagtails live year-round, securing all their food, nesting and raising their young there.

In the Black Duck study it was found that in addition to the breeding pairs in the population, there was a sizeable constituent of floaters (non-breeding, non-territorial birds) which lived on the many small irrigation dams adjoining the river. These dams enabled the floaters to survive but not breed as the dams lacked suitable nesting habitat. Floaters continually challenged the river birds for their territories and were occasionally successful, taking not only the territory but also the mate of the loser. On occasions when the Eerste River dried up, the territorial river birds were also displaced to the dams but once the river began flowing again there was a scramble for positions on it. The message is clear: in order to breed, a Black Duck needs a river territory.

Bathing is followed by a session of preening in which feather barbs are carefully stroked into position with the beak (left). During summer – their nesting season – Water Dikkops are found in pairs which are spaced at intervals along beaches and larger rivers. At other times of the year, however, they may aggregate during the day to roost communally and disperse at night to feed.

The epitome of patience, a solitary Grey Heron stands alert in thigh-deep water watching for the slightest movement that will reveal the presence of a fish. Eventually, as this sequence of photographs shows, the bird is rewarded and in a flash it lunges deep into the water to impale a luckless tilapia on its dagger-like beak. By stabbing with the mandibles held slightly open, the heron has two daggers at its disposal. It often requires more drastic treatment to immobilize large fish before they are swallowed: sometimes the heron carries them to dry ground where they are repeatedly impaled or beaten. In this particular instance the fish eventually proved too large for the bird to swallow and was abandoned. The Grey Heron found in southern Africa is the same species as that seen in England where it is known simply as the 'Heron'; it also occurs widely across Europe and Asia.

In southern Africa Goliath Herons (above) have taken readily to the innumerable man-made lakes across the subcontinent. Here a bird wings lazily across the expanse of open water created by the Allemanskraal Dam in the Orange Free State. This province alone has an estimated population of 300-400 Goliath Herons, most of them found on impoundments such as this one.

Longtailed Wagtails are the aristocracy in wagtails. The Reverend Godfrey, a perceptive birdwatcher who lived in the eastern Cape in the early part of the century, wrote in *The Blythswood Review* that they could hardly be matched 'for delicacy of colouring, grace of movement…'. Their up and down bobbing tail motion matches the ambience of their environment – the spangled movement of light and dark as water sparkles its way over and around the rocks along a forested mountain stream. The little tail-wagging bird tripping about on the rocks blends so well with its surroundings that even the stealthy African Goshawk misses it. The Palmiet wagtails were found to have a high adult survival rate, some individuals living as long as 10 years. The offspring raised each summer dispersed away from their parental territories, most never to be seen again. Unlike the Black Duck which feeds mainly on plant material, and the Halfcollared Kingfisher, which specializes in catching fish, Longtailed Wagtails take small insects like caddisfly and mayfly nymphs from the river's edge and from partly submerged rocks. But in all three species it is presumably the availability of prey in their stretches of river that determines the size of their territories. The upper reaches of rivers have been subject to the least impact and it is here that these three species are most commonly found.

Rather less is known about the habits of the elusive African Finfoot which favours the middle reaches of rivers where there is a thick fringe of overhanging vegetation. If caught unawares in open water it swims fast and low to the nearest cover and disappears into it. It is rather cormorant-like in appearance, swimming low in the water with its long neck moving back and forth in a smooth, graceful movement. However, unlike the cormorant, it does not dive and it feeds mainly on aquatic insects and frogs which it snatches with a rapid strike from the overhanging vegetation.

Three other uncommon waterbirds, the Black Stork, Whitebacked Night Heron and Pel's Fishing Owl, live mainly along rivers although none of them is entirely restricted to this habitat. Black Storks are unusual in that they probably represent a recent colonization of the subcontinent by birds originating in Europe. The same thing has happened, but less successfully, in the case of the White Stork. Black Storks occur sparsely across eastern Europe and Asia, migrating into Africa in winter. As recently as 1936 they were not known to breed on the subcontinent but in the last decade several surveys have shown that they nest widely in the region where there may be as many as 1 000 breeding pairs. They breed in winter, building an eagle-like stick nest on a cliff (in contrast to their European forebears which nest in trees), laying in May–June and fledging their chicks in October. Unlike some other stork species, Black Storks are not colonial while breeding and pairs nest at least three or four kilometres apart. They remain attached to the same nests for years and even decades although they do not breed every year, skipping in times of low river flow. In such circumstances these normally solitary birds may be forced to aggregate in places where food is still to be found. This may sometimes be at pools along rivers, or sometimes on dams.

The Pel's Fishing Owl is another mainly riverine species which, in drought conditions, may be forced to aggregate in numbers at the last remaining pools along drying rivers. In less extreme circumstances this owl is territorial and pairs are spaced along suitable riverine habitat at intervals of two or three kilometres. By day they roost in deeply shaded trees (such as *Trichilia* and *Garcinia*) and at night they move out along the river to hunt, feeding on fish which they catch from low perches overhanging the water. Their deep, penetrating hoot, audible from up to three kilometres away, is usually the only evidence of the bird's presence in an area. The Okavango's Panhandle region is considered prime fishing owl habitat and here they have been studied in some detail. Nesting takes place in winter. They lay eggs during the height of the flood in March–April so that when the chicks fledge the water is receding and fishing conditions are optimal.

Even more secretive is the third of the trio, the Whitebacked Night Heron. It is another unobtrusive, nocturnal bird that lives along thickly wooded rivers though it has not been studied in any detail and little is known of its habits or behaviour. By day the birds sit motionless in dense foliage overhanging water where they are very difficult to see; at night they venture out like the owls, to fish and catch frogs from rocks along the river. Like the owl, this species has large eyes enabling it to hunt at night and like the owl, too, river degradation has certainly contributed to its rarity.

The list of waterbirds commonly found along rivers extends to three other heron species (Goliath, Grey, Greenbacked), three shorebirds, including the numerous Common Sandpiper and rare Green Sandpiper, both non-breeding migrants from the Palearctic, the Water Dikkop and three kingfishers, the Giant, Pied and Malachite.

Standing crouched, either on a branch or a stone beside the water, is the characteristic posture of the Greenbacked Heron while fishing (above). This heron is highly adaptable, though, and is one of very few bird species known to use bait while hunting. Occasionally recorded in southern Africa, this technique has been reported more often in the Asian and American races of the species. It involves dropping a spider or insect on to the surface of the water to lure any fish within striking distance.

69

Some kingfishers come in dazzling colours: the tiny Malachite Kingfisher (right) is one of the jewels, glowing in the brilliant richness of its plumage. Found along most streams and rivers, it lives on small fish which it hunts from perches overhanging the water. Marginally less colourful is the larger Halfcollared Kingfisher (above) which is distinguished by its black bill and more turquoise-coloured upper parts. One of the few kingfisher species entirely lacking blue in its plumage is the Pied Kingfisher (below) which is seen here hovering over open water. When perches are available, Pied Kingfishers make use of them, but this bird's ability to hover in the air enables it to hunt in places that no other kingfisher can reach. On Lake Kariba, Pied Kingfishers have been found fishing over open water as much as three kilometres from the shore.

It includes only one other duck besides the African Black Duck (the Egyptian Goose), and the African Fish Eagle, common on other wetlands as well, also frequents rivers.

The list also includes the Hamerkop which is as much at home along a river as in any other aquatic habitat. These birds are oddballs – a bizarre combination of incongruities. Flying along a river, they remind one of a winged undertaker; when soaring high they look like eagles. Their raucous wailing and shrieking call is nothing short of demented and the monumental nests they build defy explanation. They feed by paddling about in shallow water, even in roadside puddles and garden ponds, always looking for frogs, crabs, fish and aquatic insects. Sometimes they do a foot shuffle in the manner of a Little Egret to flush fish; occasionally they have been seen to fly over water and plunge in and catch prey like an African Fish Eagle. One was timed eating a total of 123 dead minnows in 64 seconds! Their nests, which take three to six weeks to build and often last for years after the Hamerkops have done with them, are greatly favoured nest sites of Egyptian Geese and Barn Owls and are also appreciated by Monitor Lizards and bee swarms. The nest, a domed chamber made of sticks and mud, is about a metre in diameter with a small, down-facing entrance hole on one side. It can weigh more than 100 kilograms and can fill the back of a truck. The top of the nest is decorated with the most extraordinary accumulation of debris imaginable. For example, the inventory of material adorning the top of one found in Bulawayo was recorded as follows: one pan brush, one broken cassette tape, one glove, one plastic dish, one plastic cup, two peacock feathers, chicken feathers, two socks, rabbit fur, 45 rags, four mealie cobs, one piece of glass, four bits of wire, one plastic comb, one pair of male underpants, one typewriter ribbon, one piece of leather belt, four stockings, two pieces of tin, two pieces of foam rubber, seven pieces of hose pipe, nine pieces of electrical pipe, six pieces of asbestos roofing, 11 bones, 12 pieces of sandpaper, four pieces of insulation tape, 10 plastic bags, nine pieces of paper, 56 scraps of tinfoil, six bicycle tyres and six lengths of insulating wire! Although the nesting habits of these birds have been studied in detail, the reason for their building such huge nests has not adequately been explained: other close relatives (storks, herons) make do with simple platforms made of twigs.

The Hamerkop, with its third world taste in nesting materials and its ability to exploit a variety of aquatic habitats, is probably better able to survive the continued assault on the rivers than the other more specialized river species. For these, the prospect is bleak: an ever-increasing fragmentation of their preferred habitats, more prolonged and frequent periods of low flow and impoverished food resources as the food chain on which they depend is eroded away.

The Hamerkop's unusual profile (opposite) renders it unmistakable: even young birds barely out of the nest sport the species' unusual pony-tailed crest. Even more remarkable is the extraordinary nest built by these birds: it consists of a huge domed chamber of sticks, grass and mud with a small circular entrance on one side (top, right). The sexes share the task of building, taking about six weeks to complete a nest (above, right).

MARSHES AND
MOORHENS

*Against a backdrop of papyrus, a Great White
Egret wings up one of the Okavango's innumerable
meandering channels. Almost the size of a
Grey Heron, this species is the largest of the egrets.
The yellow colour of its beak signifies that it is
in non-breeding condition: during breeding the beak
becomes jet-black and for some time afterwards it
remains partly yellow and partly black.*

MARSH, SWAMP, BOG, SPONGE, VLEI and wetland are words that, for most people, have the same connotation: they bring to mind the image of a mosaic of squelchy ground, open water and aquatic vegetation, sedges, bulrushes, feathery-topped reedbeds and mosquitoes. The words have originated from different sources used at different times to describe different landscapes and it is no wonder that the distinctions between them are fuzzy. The term 'wetland' is the first source of confusion because of its ambiguity. It sometimes refers specifically to a vegetated marsh as defined as 'an area of waterlogged soil, dominated by emergent vegetation', but it is more generally used when referring to the whole family of aquatic systems: rivers, lakes, dams, pans and other waterbodies as well as the vegetated marshes – which is what this chapter is about.

A 'vlei' is a peculiarly South African term, an anglicized Afrikaans word which is almost as ambiguous as the word 'wetland'. The 'type specimens' are probably those wetlands first encountered by white settlers in the south-western Cape that still bear the name 'vlei' – Rondevlei, Rietvlei, Swartvlei, Zeekoeivlei, Paardevlei, Klawervlei, Vogelvlei and many others. Some of these are open lakes, others are vegetated; some are temporary and others are permanent. Many are excellent waterbird habitats. The term's usage has extended to reedswamps (Memelvlei) and to seasonal floodplains (Nylsvlei). It is useful to the extent that it provides an umbrella term for sponges (which are high altitude vleis at river sources), marshes (which are vegetated waterlogged areas with little standing water), swamps (which are similar but have a higher water table and areas of standing water), bogs (marshes sitting on an accumulation of peat) and floodplains (which are seasonally inundated margins of rivers). Vleis can also be subdivided according to their dominant plant communities; for example there are sedge vleis, reed vleis, mangrove swamps, papyrus swamps, and so on.

It is fitting to start looking at vlei birds by going to the Okavango Delta situated in northern Botswana. By far the largest southern African wetland, it is fed by the subcontinent's third largest river and is one of the natural wonders of the world. Every year in excess of 10 000 million cubic metres of water (which would form a cube measuring 2,3 kilometres square), picked up in the Angolan 'Planalto Central' highlands, drain southwards, first through the Cubango and Cuito rivers and then, after their junction, through the Kavango which meanders lazily through Caprivi into Botswana. Here it fans out into a six-fingered hand, each finger transporting the ever-diminishing water southwards over desert sands until the last trickle spills into the Botletle River and winds away towards Makgadikgadi Pan. Each year Angola's summer rains pour into the system a surge of floodwater which reaches the head of the Delta (the Panhandle) in March-April, and the Botletle at the bottom end, about two months later. As the water rises, it inundates the floodplains adjacent to the main channels, thrusting life into them before evaporation takes its toll and the water level recedes to the permanent channels awaiting the next flood. The entire labyrinth of river channels, pans, floodplains and islands covers about 1,7 million hectares, an area approaching that of the Kruger National Park. It is a constantly changing system: millions of tons of sediment come in annually, changing gradients, forcing channels to shift position, cutting off one and opening another. Rafts of papyrus do the same thing and even the trail left by a hippopotamus can trigger the water into taking a new route. It is the seasonally inundated floodplains that are the production-factories of the system and here the large concentrations of birds gather to feed on the vast numbers of barbel fingerlings and the mass of other aquatic life generated by the floodwater.

*With a pair of barbecue tongs for a beak, the African Spoonbill is well equipped
to pick up small aquatic insects in shallow water (above). It forages by wading about,
sweeping its partly submerged, partly opened beak from side to side and snapping
it closed when it makes contact with something edible. In other respects spoonbills are
much like ibises to which they are closely related. The sexes are similar in
plumage but males have longer beaks than females (opposite).*

Eighty-four fish species are found in the Delta and, as would be expected, many of the bird species are piscivorous. The African Fish Eagle is among them, its ringing call being one of the characteristic sounds of the Okavango. The Delta is partitioned into innumerable territories, each occupied by a pair of these colourful eagles, and each centres on a large stick nest placed high in a tree which is the focus of the pair's activity throughout the winter months when they breed. Storks are well represented in the Delta. For the Yellowbilled Stork this region provides its major southern African breeding ground and its egg-laying in August and September coincides with a feast of fish provided by the drying floodplains. Along with several other stork and heron species, these birds nest colonially in a few regularly used sites in 'gomoti' figs standing in water. The Darter, Reed Cormorants, Purple Herons, Squacco Herons and African Spoonbills commonly nest alongside them. Marabou Storks, which also avail themselves of the fish harvest, nest in the colonies as well, the Okavango being the only southern African locality where they breed with any regularity.

A Purple Heron is captured in the evening light in typical habitat (below). Purple Herons are invariably associated with cover and their coloration and striped necks enable them to blend well into the sedges and reeds they frequent. Solitary hunters, they do, however, nest communally on occasion when up to a dozen pairs may build their nests in the same reedbed.

Two herons for which the Delta has particular significance are the Rufousbellied Heron and the Slaty Egret. The former is a rare bird on the subcontinent and the Okavango supports most of its breeding population. The Slaty Egret is one of the Okavango's 'specials' as it is largely endemic to this area. It looks much like a Black Egret, which is also present in the Delta, but is a lighter grey in colour, has a brown throat and yellowish legs as well as feet. When originally collected in 1895 it was described as a separate species; later it was considered to be merely a colour-variant of the Black Egret but in 1971 it was again recognized as a species in its own right. One characteristic that immediately separates the two is that the Slaty Egret does not canopy-feed in the way that the Black Egret does.

Other piscivorous species include the Pied and Malachite Kingfishers. The Pied is especially common and in the Delta it is ubiquitous. Its habit, unique among the kingfishers, of hovering above the water to look for fish opens up hunting grounds to it that are unavailable to strictly perch-hunting species such as the little Malachite.

Reed Cormorants live on fish and hunt under water, diving as deep as five to six metres in pursuit of their prey (below). The Reed Cormorant's long beak is sharply hooked at its tip, so enabling the bird to maintain a firm grip on any slippery fish it may catch. The feet are set well back on the body and the toes are webbed to aid swimming under water.

After a session of fishing, cormorants climb up on to perches to dry off, as this Reed Cormorant is doing (right). Their feathers, which do not have the repellency of duck plumage, become waterlogged in the water; this reduces buoyancy and enables cormorants to dive more efficiently, but it means that they need to dry after swimming. Breeding adults have dark fronts and red eyes; this bird is probably still a youngster in its first plumage.

The Pied is proportionately much longer-winged than other kingfishers, a feature that is presumably related to its hovering behaviour. Greenbacked Herons are also common in the Delta where they live on its rich fish harvest. This species occurs almost worldwide and as many as 30 subspecies have been described, some virtually unrecognizable as the same species as the southern African birds. They have the interesting but rarely observed habit (in southern Africa) of fishing with bait. Birds that do this toss a small object – sometimes an insect or spider; at other times a twig, berry, piece of bark, a leaf or even a piece of polystyrene into the water to lure fish to the surface which they then catch.

Many non-piscivorous waterbirds also live on the Delta. Of the five or six duck species that are found here regularly the dainty little Pygmy Goose, floating among the water-lilies like a porcelain ornament, is much the commonest – in fact the Okavango population is possibly the highest concentration of these birds found anywhere in Africa. This diminutive duck has a goose-like head and beak, features that have led to its being called (erroneously) a goose. The strong beak serves it well in opening the water lily seeds that are its main food. Its common occurrence in the Delta is probably due to an abundance of these water lilies and an abundance of safe nest sites provided by the innumerable holes found in the tall mopane trees fringing the channels and pans.

An almost obligate companion of the Pygmy Goose in the rafts of water lilies is another striking bird: the African Jacana, an unusual shorebird which has evolved enormously long toes and toenails – proportionately longer, in fact, than those of any other bird species. These enable it to walk on floating vegetation with absolute impunity and, while tripping about on the broad leaves, to feed on aquatic insects that live at the water surface. The African Jacana is a characteristic bird of floodplains since water lilies rapidly colonize these systems when they flood. They are boisterous, rowdy birds that make loud, shrieking calls and seem to spend most of their time chasing one another. They are among a select handful of polyandrous species, females mating with successive males, laying clutches of eggs for each, and leaving them to incubate these without assistance. Males are territorial and much of their squabbling is to do with asserting their territorial rights or with shouting to attract the attention of the female of the moment. Females fight among one another for supremacy of males, staking out 'super-territories' which embrace those of several males for which they lay eggs. A single female can lay up to ten clutches in a season, either for successive males or as replacements for males that lose earlier clutches. The nests are skimpy pads of waterweed, barely capable of supporting the four beautifully marked eggs and egg losses are very high. There are various explanations for the African Jacana's unusual mating system. The most convincing is that it is a response to high clutch losses; the female's emancipation from its parental duties enables it to spend more time feeding and thus to build up condition for re-laying more quickly. Once such a system is entrenched, females lay subsequent clutches for whom they like, and not just for their original partner.

The tiny, retiring Lesser Jacana, which is hardly recognizable as a relative of its brash and noisy larger cousin, is also found in the Okavango. It is a rare bird on the subcontinent and the Delta is virtually the only wetland here where it is consistently present. It seldom ventures into open lily fields but prefers areas of flooded grass. Its nest is an even skimpier version of the African Jacana's nest and its eggs are tiny replicas of those of the larger species. Lesser Jacanas are not polyandrous and pairs remain together to share all parental duties. A crucial difference is that the Lesser Jacana's eggs, perhaps because of their smaller size and the exposed nature of the nest, need almost constant parental attendance.

Darters differ from cormorants in that they have straight, dagger-like beaks on which they impale their prey. They live almost entirely on fish, hunting them by swimming under water in the manner of a cormorant. Often seen with only their long, thin necks exposed above the surface, they are sometimes known as 'snakebirds'. Darters also have large, duck-like, webbed feet (above).

*The Squacco is one of the smaller and more
furtive heron species. It hunts by stalking its prey
among the emergent plants in shallow water where its
streaked plumage enables it to blend well with its
surroundings. By contrast, it becomes conspicuous when
it flies and reveals its starched white wings. In breeding
condition, Squacco Herons acquire long white nape
plumes and a rich turquoise colour at the base of the
beak (below), a feature lacking in non-breeding birds
(right). The shaggy head feathers normally lie flat, but
when the Squacco is threatened or frightened (right)
these can be raised to form a fearsome-looking ruff.*

This can only be achieved if both parents co-operate; in contrast, African Jacana eggs are attended for less than half the day and much of their incubation is done by the sun.

Almost alongside the Okavango Delta, but lying north of it, is an intricate web of floodplains, lagoons and channels fed by the Kwando and Zambezi rivers which bring water into the system from the north-west and north-east respectively. They are linked by the Chobe River into which water is pushed back by the Zambezi during its March-April flood. In the centre of the web lies Lake Liambezi, often dry but sometimes a 10 000-hectare expanse of water surrounded by a vast wetland area in which perhaps 20 per cent of the eastern Caprivi is inundated. Although the same mix of waterbirds as occurs in the Okavango is found here, some species are of particular interest. For example, the rare Pinkbacked Pelican chooses Lake Liambezi as one of only two or three breeding sites in southern Africa. Another scarce bird which is well represented is the Longtoed Plover, an unusual shorebird that, rather like the jacana, lives on mats of floating vegetation. Two small warblers, the Greater Swamp Warbler (in the papyrus swamp) and the Chirping Cisticola, are common in these wetlands but are found nowhere else in southern Africa. The Caprivi floodplains almost link the Okavango with the very extensive wetlands found in Zambia. These support more than half the world's population of the rare Wattled Crane, some of which move into Botswana and Caprivi during high floods in Zambia. It is curious that the eccentric-looking African Shoebill of central Africa, a tall stork-like bird with a huge bill, has not colonized the Okavango.

The African Jacana lays the most exquisitely marked clutch of eggs on the most precarious of nests (right). An incautious approach could tilt the platform and cause an egg to roll off and be lost. Here a male carefully decides where to place its feet as it approaches the nest to incubate.

*Female African Jacanas are larger and more aggressive than males and dominate
them in most situations. Thus, during the courtship sequence (above) which takes place
on the rudimentary nest, the female (on the right) adopts a submissive head-down
posture so as not to intimidate the male in the build-up to copulation.
If she did not do this, he would be reluctant to get too close.*

At close quarters the dark, sleek Glossy Ibis shows an iridescent coat. Non-breeding birds (left) are streaked with white about the head and neck; in full breeding plumage this area becomes a glossy bronze and the lores a vivid blue (above). Nestlings are unusual in having two pale vertical candy stripes across their otherwise dark beaks. Often found in groups, Glossy Ibises forage in shallow water in marshy situations, using their long, tapering beaks to probe for and catch aquatic insects, frogs and crustaceans. Of the four ibis species occurring in southern Africa, the Glossy Ibis is the most restricted to aquatic habitats.

Throwing caution to the winds, a Moorhen swims across an open pond (above).
Although less shy than rails and crakes, this species likes to have cover close at hand
so that it can disappear into it at the first sign of danger. Apart from the
waxy red and yellow beak, the Moorhen's most visible feature is the white patch
which is revealed each time the tail is flicked. The more agitated the bird,
the more frequently it exposes its undertail coverts.

Further north in Africa it lives in papyrus swamps and it is numerous in the Bengwuelu Swamp in Zambia. It subsists on a variety of aquatic fauna but especially on barbel and lungfish and it has been suggested that the absence of lungfish in the Okavango system has prevented this bird's successful colonization of this wetland.

Other floodplains occur in southern Africa but they are dwarfed by the size of the Okavango and Caprivi systems. In Zululand, the Mkuze River forms an 18 000-hectare floodplain of lagoons, channels, papyrus- and reed-swamps before it enters Lake St Lucia. North of it, in Tongaland, the Pongolo River spills over its levees and inundates some 35 pans that fringe it in an area covering about 12 000 hectares. This happens to a greater or lesser extent every summer, although the building of the Jozini Dam upstream from the floodplain has essentially replaced the natural flow regime with an artificial one in which planned water-releases from the dam attempt to simulate natural conditions. The well-known birding locality, Ndumo Game Reserve, straddles the lower end of this floodplain. Further north in Mozambique, along the coastal plain, there are floodplains associated with the Inkomati, Limpopo, Sabie, Pungwe and other rivers, while the Zambezi River fans into a large, seasonally flooded delta where it meets the sea. All these floodplain localities are vitally important breeding areas and drought refugia for ducks and other waterbirds.

The Nyl River floodplain in the central Transvaal is a well-known birdwatching venue; it floods, on average, once every three years, when up to 16 000 hectares become inundated and the mosaic of flooded rice grass, pans with water lilies, reedbeds and flooded acacia savanna attract a great diversity of waterbirds. Openwater birds like flamingos and pelicans are rare vagrants here, but herons, ducks, crakes and rails are well represented and up to 80 000 birds of 103 waterbird species (grebes to terns) have been recorded. In such years the Nyl supports the largest breeding populations of Great White Egrets, Black Egrets and Squacco Herons in southern Africa and it is one of very few known breeding localities of the rare Bittern on the subcontinent. It is also a major venue for crakes, rails and flufftails and literally thousands of Lesser Gallinules and Lesser Moorhens, both tropical migrants, nest here in the floods.

All these floodplain-type wetlands draw their water from catchments situated away from the wetland itself, in some cases from hundreds of kilometres away. For this reason there is a certain amount of predictability in their flooding regime and in the very large Okavango and Chobe systems flooding occurs, to a greater or lesser extent, every year. By contrast, scattered across the subcontinent there are ephemeral wetlands based on pan systems which have no external drainage and rely on exceptionally heavy rain falling *in situ* to inundate them. Some of these remain openwater pans with bare shorelines and are described in the next chapter; others have the vegetation characteristics of floodplains. The most extensive of these lies west of the Okavango in Bushmanland, Namibia, where two extensive panveld areas cover about 120 000 hectares. The pans are not river-fed and are only infrequently inundated. However, when heavy rains do fall here, as happened in 1988–89, this otherwise dry landscape is transformed into a place of magic. Large numbers of ducks, of which the Redbilled Teal is the most common, move into the area; flocks of Openbilled Storks arrive and establish nesting colonies; flamingos and Black-necked Grebes move on to the more saline pans that are devoid of vegetation; clouds of Whiskered Terns appear from nowhere and the grassy pans fill with an array of crakes, rails, moorhens and gallinules. This is one of the few localities in southern Africa where a rare migrant from northern Europe, the Great Snipe, has been seen in recent years. The

In appearance similar to a dark version of the Little Egret, this Black Egret (top) shows off its gaudy yellow toes. Unlike the Little Egret, however, it has a distinctive and unusual fishing technique (above) in which it spreads its wings over the water to form a canopy. This behaviour is thought to lure small fish into the shade where they can be easily caught by the bird.

Not geese at all, Pygmy Geese derive their name from the goose-like shape of their bills. They feed mainly on water lily seeds and the strong, blunt beak may be adapted for this purpose. Here a female (above right) shows the duller markings of her sex. Females undertake all the incubation but both parents attend the young after hatching.

highlight in 1989 was the colonization here by a breeding population of Slaty Egrets. They may have been displaced from the Okavango by the exceptionally high water conditions prevailing there as, in the same year, these birds were also recorded in Zimbabwe and the Transvaal, both sites far out of their normal range.

East of the Okavango, in Zimbabwe, lies a similar but smaller panveld area. The northern part of the Hwange National Park is studded with pans of all sizes which lie dry for years; then, following exceptionally high rains, they are transformed into a rich wetland. This happened, for example, in 1984–85 when the pans filled virtually overnight and were rapidly colonized by large numbers of waterfowl, among them the transcontinental migrants, the Lesser Moorhen and Dwarf Bittern.

Other less extensive panveld wetlands of this type which lack external sources of water exist in the northern Kruger National Park (Wambiya Pans), along the Zululand coast (Bangazi Plain), in the western Transvaal (Steenbokpan), and elsewhere.

In the higher rainfall interior of South Africa there are many examples of sponges, reed swamps, sedge swamps and other similar wetlands. Many have been degraded to varying extents through abusive land-use practices and some have disappeared entirely. The once-famous Potchefstroom marshes, where the first Whitewinged Flufftail was collected, were drained decades ago to make way for housing, and many of the East Griqualand upland marshes, made known to ornithology by the bird-artist Finch-Davies, have gone. Some of the wetlands have been drained, some have been dammed, others simply destroyed by erosion resulting from over-grazing and the waterbirds most

The male Pygmy Goose, with his delicately patterned face and waxy yellow bill,
is a most attractive waterfowl (above). Despite their rich coloration, males are not easily
detected among the maze of water lilies to which they are so attached. When startled,
they rise rapidly from the water and fly with quick wing beats, uttering a squeaky
whistle in the process.

dependent on these habitats have declined accordingly. The Wattled Crane, ranked as an endangered bird in South Africa, is dependent on these upland marshes and its range has been greatly reduced here.

Although the scorecard shows an unquestionable net loss of wetlands of this type, fortunately there have been gains in some quarters. Given water and the right topography, such wetlands are easily created: the Witwatersrand, for example, is decked with a string of wetlands that did not exist a century ago. This most densely populated region on the subcontinent consumes a great amount of water (about one thousand million cubic metres per annum) of which about two thirds is returned to the rivers as effluent, usually enriched with nutrients. Much of this water does not originate in the region but is pumped in from distant catchments to meet the demand. Basin transfer of water from the Tugela catchment in Natal has been operational for a decade and future developments include an even larger transfer scheme from Lesotho.

The rivers draining south from the Witwatersrand – the Klipspruit, Blesbokspruit and Natalspruit – enriched in nutrients and swelled by imported water, have been transformed from conventional channelled rivers into wide expanses of reedbed interspersed with open water, in places teeming with coots, ducks and even flamingos. Large breeding colonies of Cattle Egrets (exploiting the many dairy herds), Sacred Ibis (living off the pig farms) and other more conventional waterbirds have become established in these reedbeds and they are an undoubted environmental asset to the community. In 1950 Glossy Ibises, never previously known to breed in Africa and always regarded as a non-breeding visitor from the Northern Hemisphere, were for the first time found nesting in such a colony on the Witwatersrand. Since then they have become firmly established, more than 500 pairs having nested here since 1974. Another colonist, living on refuse dumps and by begging at road houses, is the Greyheaded Gull: more than half the population of this species in southern Africa now probably breeds in this area.

Sewage works serve the various towns in the Pretoria-Witwatersrand-Vereeniging region (as they do most other towns in southern Africa) and where these include natural settling dams in their process, numerous highly productive vleis have been created and are being maintained. Many of these sites have been developed as bird sanctuaries and attract great numbers of visitors, both human and avian. From the vantage-point of a hide at almost any one of them, it is possible to watch Purple Gallinules emerge from the reeds and munch away like parrots on tender plant stems, to witness Great Crested Grebes performing their elaborate courtship or to see Ethiopian Snipe shuffling along the muddy edges, probing their long beaks deep into the sludge.

In breeding plumage, Yellowbilled Storks almost glow in the light of the evening sun (opposite). Their normally white plumage acquires a rosy hue; their backs are dappled with pink and their legs and face become an enriched red. These large storks are usually gregarious and forage, roost and nest in groups. They hunt in shallow water, wading about and seeking food with beak opened and partly submerged. Prey is quickly snapped up when encountered.

CHAPTER

5

LIVING

AT THE EDGE

*The Redbilled Teal (left) is rated as the most
abundant duck in southern Africa. Gregarious and
fast-flying, it moves widely about the subcontinent's
wetlands in response to changing conditions. The tiny
size of the Hottentot Teal (bottom left corner) is most
apparent when it is seen in flight alongside Redbilled
Teals. Each of these 'dabbling ducks' has a distinctively
coloured speculum (secondary feathers in the wing),
shown to good effect in flight as is seen here.*

OPEN WATER AND BARE SHORELINES are the uncomplicated, two-dimensional habitats that lie at one end of a wetland continuum: at the other end are the wetlands in which the water can't be seen for the plants. Open water and bare shorelines occur in all aquatic habitats to some extent – along rivers, in vleis, floodplains and even, in a minor way, in reed- and papyrus-swamps. But they are most characteristic of lakes, dams, pans, estuaries and lagoons, and there are numerous waterbird species that are essentially restricted to these environments.

Southern Africa has relatively few natural lakes. Virtually all of these are to be found along the subcontinent's coastal plain and they owe their origins to once having been estuaries. Many, like Lake St Lucia, are functionally still estuaries that open to the sea and are subject to its salinity and tidal influence. Although sometimes called lakes (as St Lucia is), they are more properly termed estuaries. Others have changed to lakes as, over the centuries, they have become landlocked by the seaward expansion of the coastline. Most lie along the Mozambique coastal plain; some are in Zululand (for example, Lake Sibayi) and there are a few, such as the Wilderness lakes, in the southern Cape. The arid interior has been particularly unaccommodating in creating lakes, although the artefacts of vast inland waters from bygone eras are still to be found in the form of huge, dry saltpans. Little-known Lake Fundudzi in Venda is one of southern Africa's few natural inland lakes; it was created about 500 years ago by a landslide which dammed the Mutale River much as a man-made dam would have done.

Deficient in natural waterbodies though the interior may be, there are a great many man-made lakes spread across the subcontinent. Almost every river in the region has been dammed, some more than 500 times between source and sea. In 1980 half a million farm dams were estimated to exist in South Africa alone besides more than 500 large state dams. These have been built to provide a stable supply of water for towns and industry, irrigation and power-generation and their impact on the rivers has often been catastrophic. Yet these dams have created more than a million hectares of open, often permanent, freshwater habitat that did not exist before. Kariba Dam, built on the Zambezi River in 1958, took over four years to fill and is one of the largest man-made lakes in the world. Virtually an inland sea, it is 30 kilometres wide and 290 kilometres long with a surface area (440 000 hectares) exceeding that of all South Africa's dams combined. Further downstream, in Mozambique, lies the somewhat smaller Cahora Bassa Dam (274 000 hectares). These two dams dwarf every other permanent waterbody on the subcontinent, whether man-made or natural. The next largest are the Hendrik Verwoerd Dam (which has a surface area of 36 000 hectares), the Vaal Dam (29 000 hectares) and Bloemhof Dam (23 000 hectares).

The terms 'dam' and 'lake' are often used interchangeably; Kariba and Cahora Bassa, for example, are today usually referred to as Lake Kariba and Lake Cahora Bassa. However, usage of the word 'dam' is firmly entrenched when referring to practically all South Africa's man-made lakes. Their names were chosen without the thought of 'lake' being appended and, although Allemanskraal Dam, Bronkhorstspruit Dam and hundreds of other similar names sound reasonable, none is likely to make the change to the technically more correct Lake Pataskloof or Lake Koos Raubenheimer. Strictly speaking, 'dam' refers to the wall that holds back the water while the body of water itself is the lake (or impoundment, or, in England, referred to as the reservoir). While calling these waterbodies 'dams' may be a misnomer, the word 'dam' does carry with it the information that they are man-made.

Redbilled Teals forage by dipping, by submerging their heads in the water while swimming (above) or by 'upending' (opposite). Like other dabblers, they do not generally dive for food but may do this to escape predators while they are in flightless moult. The sexes are similar in plumage but can be distinguished by subtle head features: females have a steeper sloping forehead than males and the black upper ridge on her bill may be less distinct.

In southern Africa a third term – pan – sows further confusion. Pans are shallow, usually circular or oval depressions in the landscape that fill with water during rains. They are characteristic of flat landscapes; are not fed by, or connected to, rivers in most cases and are often found in clusters. The panveld area centring on Lake Chrissie in the eastern Transvaal, for example, has 294 pans of this kind dotted over an area of 50 000 hectares. Here the largest pans in the system (which carry water for the longest periods) are referred to locally as lakes and the smaller, more ephemeral ones, as pans. There are many such panveld areas scattered across the subcontinent. They are especially prevalent in the arid interior and, because of the low and erratic rainfall in this region, they seldom fill with water. The largest pans on the subcontinent, each covering more than a half million hectares, are Etosha Pan in Namibia and, in Botswana, Makgadikgadi with its eastern (Sua Pan) and western (Ntwetwe Pan) limbs. Both of these are salt pans that rarely fill completely but become inundated to varying degrees when runoff from the Ekuma and Nata rivers (respectively) reaches them. They both belong to wetter eras when they were vast natural lakes connected to major drainage systems. Ngami is another large pan (20 000 hectares) which stands dry for years and even decades, then fills briefly when overflow water from the Okavango Delta reaches it. Clearly Livingstone did not have the perspective of its being a dustbowl more often than a lake when he discovered it in 1849 and named it Lake Ngami. No other pans reach these dimensions and most are no more than a few hectares in extent.

Lastly, there are lagoons – or what are referred to as lagoons – on the subcontinent. Langebaan Lagoon, stretching over 6 000 hectares, is the largest of these; it is a large shallow-water arm of the sea protected by the Churchhaven peninsula but subject to tides and having the salinity of seawater. Walvis Bay and Sandwich Harbour in Namibia are lagoons of the same type and there are many smaller ones. Their great significance lies in the large numbers of shorebirds dependent on them.

The shorebirds, dominated by plovers and scolopacids, make up a high proportion of the waterbird species that favour openwater-cum-shore habitats. These small wading birds live at the interface between water and land; they have long legs that enable them to run along the edges or walk in shallow water and beaks designed to probe or glean insects from the mud. Two-thirds of the shorebird species are non-breeding visitors that spend half their year in southern Africa and half commuting to and from, and at their Arctic breeding grounds. Each summer they pour into the former region in great numbers, settling at the open wetlands, filling the shallows with activity as they feed and jostle with one another for space. The first arrivals, usually Greenshanks and Wood Sandpipers, start arriving indecently early at the end of July, long before winter has been laid to rest. Soon afterwards, flocks of Ruffs, Little Stints, Curlew Sandpipers and others swell the ranks. Six or seven species can be seen feeding side by side at many wetlands and 20 000 or more birds congregate at the premier sites, most of which are in the lagoons, bays, estuaries and river mouths along the west coast. The highest counts of migrant waders made in southern Africa are from Sandwich Harbour (Namibia) where more than 100 000 birds, mostly Curlew Sandpipers, Little Stints and Sanderlings, may congregate at times during their northward migration. Langebaan Lagoon regularly supports more than 50 000 birds and Walvis Bay, more than 30 000. Although they present a wonderful sight, and the largest concentrations of migrant waders to be seen in southern Africa, there are even more spectacular wintering areas further north in Africa: a staggering two million waders, for example, have been counted in Mauritania's Banc d'Arguin.

Three transglobal commuters that nest in the Arctic and over-winter in southern Africa. Smallest of the trio is the 25 gram Little Stint (opposite, left top) which feeds on the muddy shoreline, seldom entering water that is more than a few centimetres in depth. As its short beak would suggest, it secures its prey by picking it up from the surface rather than by probing. Here the bird is seen stirring the water with its foot – a common shorebird technique for finding food. The Ruff (opposite, left bottom) is larger and longer-legged and wades in deeper water; the female shown here weighs about 100 grams. The 200 gram Greenshank (main photograph) is still larger and its long legs enable it to forage in water of even greater depth. It is a solitary feeder, preying on a variety of aquatic organisms including small fish which it catches by darting into shoals.

The great attraction of the west coast to migrant waders has been attributed to the offshore Benguela upwelling which makes rich fishing grounds of these coastal waters; large numbers of cormorants and other fish-eating birds live on this abundant food source and they in turn enrich with nutrients the shoreline which they frequent. As one of the end-consumers in the food chain, shorebirds are thus also major beneficiaries of the upwelling. This does not mean, though, that the rest of southern Africa lacks shorebirds. Lake St Lucia, with its very extensive mudflats and shallows, is another of their major habitats where up to 50 000 Palearctic waders have been counted. A little further to the south Richard's Bay forms another important wader site and is a regular venue for rare vagrants such as the Broadbilled Sandpiper and Redshank. Between Zululand and the west coast lie innumerable estuaries, river mouths and lagoons of varying sizes and each provides a winter refuge for lesser numbers of these tireless migrants. For example, the small estuary at the mouth of the Kowie River at Port Alfred supports up to a dozen Greenshanks in summer and many of the same individuals return here faithfully year after year. In 1977 eight Greenshanks were colour-ringed at Kowie mouth; five of them came back the next summer and four returned the following three summers. One of the eight offered a rare glimpse into the Greenshank's prodigious twice-annual migration: it was recovered in the Arctic, 10 752 kilometres away from Port Alfred.

The Wood Sandpiper (opposite) derives its name from its habitat in its Northern Hemisphere breeding grounds. Here it lives in swampy ground in the taiga, even using old nests built in trees by other birds – something unusual in shorebirds. During its six-months' sojourn in southern Africa it is the most widespread of the Palearctic shorebirds and is found on every aquatic habitat from puddles to large lakes. In terms of numbers, though, the Curlew Sandpiper (left) is probably more abundant, with the southern African population estimated at 114 000 birds.

The young Egyptian Goose (above) shows the typical
strongly patterned downy plumage of the species.
Young ducks and geese are highly precocious creatures:
they leave the nest within a day of hatching and are
immediately capable of swimming and fending for
themselves. Breeding pairs of Egyptian Geese are
extremely aggressive and belligerently drive others of
their kind out of their established territories. Sometimes
this behaviour involves active pursuit of the trespasser;
on other occasions simply spreading the wings (and so
revealing the conspicuous white forewing) is a signal of
intent sufficient to repel a would-be intruder (right).

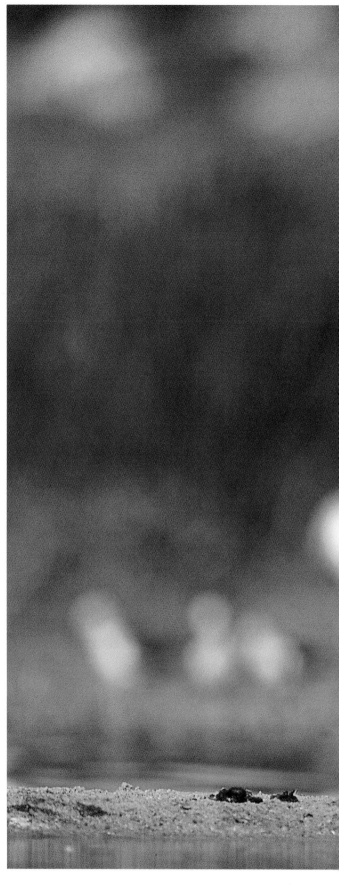

Many of the migrant shorebirds (for example, the Greenshank, Curlew Sandpiper and Little Stint) frequent both inland and coastal wetlands: some, such as the Sanderling and Turnstone, are found exclusively on coastal wetlands and others (for example, the Wood Sandpiper and Common Sandpiper) occur exclusively on inland waters. Those dependent on inland waters must, of necessity, be more flexible because of the greater changeability in the conditions of these venues. The pans, for example, provide prime shorebird habitat when they contain water but they are often dry and the birds using them one summer must move elsewhere in another year. Some of the man-made dams offer excellent shorebird habitat but many are hostile places for shorebirds because of their steep-sloping edges and the rapidly changing water-level.

In contrast to the large number of migrant species that seasonally use the shores of lakes, pans and estuaries, the contingent of resident breeding species found here is small: there are only four species, three small sandplovers and the larger Blacksmith Plover. All four live at the water's edge, dividing the shoreline into breeding territories during winter and early summer when they nest and forming scattered, nomadic flocks for the remainder of the year. The elegant little Chestnutbanded Plover is the most specific in its choice of habitat and most restricted in its occurrence. It chooses the shores of highly saline waterbodies and consequently has a fragmented range, occurring in greatest numbers on the west coast pans and on Makgadikgadi Pan. The commoner Kittlitz's Plover is usually found alongside it but it also occurs widely at non-saline waterbodies, its only requirement being a shoreline that is flat and bare. Threebanded Plovers are yet more catholic in their choice of habitat since they also range along rivers and streams where there are sandbars and bare shores. Each of these species nests in an open situation not far from the water's edge, making a small scrape in which they lay their cryptically marked clutch of two eggs. Kittlitz's Plover has the unusual habit of covering its eggs with soil when it leaves the nest. It does this with a quick foot-shuffling action as it departs, leaving the eggs invisible to a predator.

The larger, longer-legged Blacksmith Plover, one of the commonest and most widespread of birds found at the water's edge in southern Africa, also favours bare shorelines but is more tolerant of marshy conditions than the sandplovers. Now frequently seen in the wetlands of the south-western Cape, Blacksmith Plovers have colonized this region only in the past 50 years: the first-ever sighting of the species here occurred in 1939 and it first nested here in 1947. It is likely to be found on almost every farm dam that has a bare shoreline and it was perhaps the spread of dams across the Karoo that provided the stepping stones for its colonization of the south-western Cape. When nesting, it is intolerant of other shorebirds in the vicinity and the off-duty bird spends much of its time chasing the Ruff, stints, sandpipers and sandplovers from the area. It lays a larger clutch, usually of four eggs, than the sandplovers and nests close to the water's edge, often choosing an animal's hoof-print in the mud for its site.

Frequently shorebirds are simply called 'waders' but the distinction between the two has been made here because the term 'wader' also includes large wading species such as herons and egrets, storks, spoonbills and flamingos. Because of their longer legs these birds usually wade in deeper water and most prey on fish, amphibia and larger invertebrates rather than on the worms, molluscs, crustacea, fly larvae and other items favoured by the smaller shorebirds. The African Openbill is an unusual member of the large waders in that its speciality is hard-shelled prey, particularly freshwater snails and mussels. It is found erratically in southern Africa, and breeds more erratically on the subcontinent,

A gallery of sandplovers (opposite). These small, plump, short-legged shorebirds live at the water's edge, sometimes alongside one another but more usually segregated according to their individual habitat preferences. The southern African population of the Chestnutbanded Plover (top, left) centres on the Makgadikgadi Pan system in Botswana but found much more widely is the Kittlitz's Plover (top, right). The immature bird illustrated here lacks the distinctive white throat, brow and nape of the adult. The nesting behaviour of this bird is unique: it conceals its eggs by kicking material over them before it leaves the nest. The Threebanded Plover (main photograph) has a more elongated appearance than the first two species because of its much longer tail. Unlike some of the longer billed shorebirds which probe into the mud and use touch to locate prey, these sandplovers are visual hunters and glean their food from or near the water-surface.

106

generally only in those years of exceptionally high rainfall when there is widespread inundation. Flocks of these birds then home in on areas where receding water has exposed beds of mussels which provide it with an abundant food source. As many as 2 000 African Openbills have been recorded in such situations on the Zambezi floodplains in eastern Caprivi.

The food and feeding methods of flamingos are quite different from those of the storks, but these, too, rely on the years of exceptionally high rainfall to provide them with suitable breeding grounds. Although numerically abundant (for example, in southern Africa counts of the two species have exceeded one million birds), the Greater and Lesser Flamingos are surely among the most vulnerable of all waterbirds. In southern Africa, Lesser Flamingos breed only on Etosha and Sua pans and only in those years when sufficient water has flowed into them to provide a reservoir that will last the duration of the breeding cycle. The Greater Flamingo is subject to similar constraints: these two pans also provide its only regular breeding grounds on the subcontinent but, unlike the Lesser Flamingo, it has also attempted to nest at a few other localities. In the past 40 years it has twice nested on Lake St Lucia, twice on pans in the northern Cape, three times (in successive years) at De Hoop Vlei and once on a pan in the Orange Free State. Often the water recedes before the completion of the breeding cycle, leaving flocks of flightless chicks wandering aimlessly about the dry pan in searing heat while their parents commute 50 or 100 kilometres to the nearest water to feed. Mortality is extremely high in these circumstances. In the rare good years as, for example, occurred in 1971 on Etosha Pan, or in 1974 on Sua Pan (when 1,4 million Lesser and 300 000 Greater Flamingos gathered to breed), tens of thousands of young may be reared. These young must then survive perhaps a decade before the next viable breeding opportunity is presented. After nesting, the flamingos disperse across the subcontinent, those from Etosha moving to the

To rise into the air always seems to involve great effort for Spurwinged Geese (opposite, above) as they are heavy birds and the whoosh of their wings is audible from a long way off. They compound the sense of great exertion by uttering a wheezy squeak – 'chewit, chewit, chewit' – while flying, as if gasping for air. In fact, they fly a great deal and commute daily between foraging and loafing areas. Males sometimes have a knob on the forehead (opposite, below) but this feature is more common among the north African race of the species. The amount of white in the plumage also varies and northern birds have more of it on the head than the Zululand bird illustrated here eating a water lily tuber. During the breeding season the Greyheaded Gull (above) assumes an elegant grey hood which, at other times of the year, is reduced to a smudgy fragment.

west coast and down to the southern Cape, while Makgadikgadi birds probably move south-east. After a successful breeding cycle, the woolly, grey-coloured juveniles, which seem barely capable of flight, are to be seen with flocks of adults on many of the Transvaal highveld's pans. It is one of nature's best-kept secrets as to how the flamingos know when Makgadikgadi or Etosha, lying hundreds of kilometres away to the north across a water-less landscape, has water and is waiting for them. But somehow they do, and the night skies between Walvis Bay and Etosha fill with the goose-like honking of the flamingos as they make the pilgrimage to their breeding place.

Lake St Lucia is an important wetland for flamingos but it is even more important for White Pelicans, another colonial nester that needs an inaccessible place where it can breed undisturbed. Bird and Lane islands in the lake offer this, and the 1 000–1 500 pairs that nest here form the largest breeding population on the subcontinent. Fewer than 200 pairs regularly nest elsewhere, using Dassen Island off the west coast and the man-made guano platform off Walvis Bay most frequently. On rare occasions they have also attempted to nest on other offshore islands, on Etosha and Makgadikgadi pans, on Lake Ngami and on an island in Hardap Dam in Namibia, but conditions at these places seldom lead to successful breeding. Although the St Lucia pelicans obtain some of their food from the lake itself, most of their fishing is done 100 kilometres away in the pans that form the Pongolo River floodplain. The nesting birds commute daily from the lake to these fishing grounds, leaving in the morning, soaring high and sailing north on their great wings, and returning later in the day with a crop full of food for their young. Their nesting (from June to October) is timed to coincide with the dry-down on the floodplain when fish are more easy to catch, and with the emergence of islands resulting from the dropping water level. Breeding is occasionally thwarted by unseasonal rains flooding the islands or by a collapse in the fish supply. Outside of the breeding season the pelicans disperse widely on to the coastal lakes of Mozambique and the interior.

The world's largest tern, the Caspian, also breeds on the islands in Lake St Lucia, its cycle triggered by the same stimuli as affect the White Pelican. Like the pelican, it is piscivorous and it also nests on the ground where it needs an inaccessible site to breed successfully. Thus it also nests here in winter when the risk of flooding on the islands is minimal and fishing conditions are optimal. The St Lucia breeding population (about 100 pairs) is the largest in southern Africa; other colonies are situated on offshore islands (in Algoa Bay, for example) and a few pairs nest from time to time on inland waters such as Barberspan and the Vaal Dam.

Two bird species have, for different reasons, benefited tremendously from the spread of man-made dams across the subcontinent. It seems incredible, but a century ago, when Thomas Ayres compiled his checklist of the birds of the Transvaal, the fish-eating Whitebreasted Cormorant went unrecorded. Today every large dam in the province has a breeding colony of these birds and some waterbodies support more than a hundred pairs. Many nestlings have been ringed over the years at Barberspan, which harbours one of the larger breeding colonies of these cormorants, and subsequent recoveries of these show a very wide dispersal across southern Africa from the southern Cape to Zambia. This species' success is directly attributable to the proliferation of dams which provide a rich, stable food resource and safe nesting sites in trees partly submerged in the water. The building of large irrigation dams, too, has enabled Whitebreasted Cormorants to spread into the heart of the Karoo where they could never have existed previously. It is curious, though, that it took two decades before this species colonized Lake Kariba: the lake first

Not so much a waterbird as a species frequenting damp ground, the Wattled Plover (below) is easily identified by its yellow wattles. It is a noisy and conspicuous bird in early summer, the season when it pairs off to breed; at other times of the year it is found in scattered groups foraging in places where the grass has been grazed down.

*A common species that is found on most southern African water bodies, the
aptly-named Yellowbilled Duck (above) is in its behaviour similar to the Northern
Hemisphere Mallard. In fact, in areas in South Africa where Mallards have
been artificially introduced, the two species hybridize – which may prove a threat
to the viability of Yellowbill populations in future.*

filled with water in 1963; the first Whitebreasted Cormorant that was recorded on the lake was in 1982 and breeding first occurred three years after this date. White Pelicans took even longer to discover the lake. They were seen here for the very first time in 1986, 23 years after the lake filled.

The Redknobbed Coot is another success story for the dam-makers. There is scarcely a dam, from farm dam to Lake Kariba, on which this species is not present; many support hundreds of birds and the highest tally of coots on a single waterbody exceeds 45 000! Coots are vegetarians and they eat submerged aquatic plants such as *Potamogeton pectinatus* by simply dipping their heads into the water and pulling out their food. Coot numbers on dams correlate well with the size of the submerged plant crop, and the plant crop, in turn, is dependent on the nutrient level of the water. A great many dams (and other waterbodies) have been enriched to varying degrees by agricultural fertilizers and other nutrients draining into them, a process called eutrophication, and many of these are rapidly colonized by *Potamogeton* to the fishermen's disgust but coot's delight. Although coots look barely capable of sustained flight, they are inveterate travellers across the night skies and they find newly filled dams with unerring predictability. Ringing has shown that they commute up and down the subcontinent; one was even sighted in the open sea 15 kilometres offshore of Durban, reaffirming the adage 'as crazy as a coot'.

Less crazy are the ducks and geese that use the openwater habitats. Dams have eliminated the risk of being a duck on an arid subcontinent. First, they provide the ducks with drought refuges, places where they can at least survive, if not enjoy life to the full, until the return of the rain and its recharge of their ephemeral wetland breeding grounds. Secondly, the dams provide them with places where they can become flightless in safety for the 30-40 day duration of their moult. As many as 9 000 Spurwinged Geese gather for this purpose on the 6 700 hectare Sterkfontein Dam in the Orange Free State which was built to store water being transferred from the Tugela to the Witwatersrand. Many other dams support flocks of thousands of Egyptian Geese as well as South African Shelduck: 70 per cent of all shelducks gather to moult on the Free State's man-made dams – up to 5 000 on Allemanskraal Dam alone. Barberspan, in the western Transvaal, is another important waterfowl moult site which has been made more attractive to them following the diversion into it of water from the nearby Harts River.

Thus, while the rivers and their fauna wither away and the estuaries become land-locked or increasingly saline from the lack of river water, the coots, ducks and cormorants are riding high, assisted through their difficult times by the sea of water that is stored inland by all southern Africa's many dams.

Endemic to southern Africa is the South African Shelduck which has a range that centres on the Karoo. Males differ from females (opposite) in that they lack the white head markings. These colourful ducks are found in pairs on most Karoo farm dams. The two red knobs on the forehead of the Redknobbed Coot (above, right) are visible only at close range, except during the breeding season when they swell and become far more noticeable.

WATERBIRDS

AT RISK

*Piggy-backing over one another, a majestic flock of
White Pelicans gathers at a feeding site. This
gregarious species often feeds communally, the birds
driving shoals forward by swimming in lines and
so concentrating the fish in shallow water where they
can be easily caught. The impact on fish populations by
pelican flocks can be considerable and the birds often
travel long distances to find rewarding foraging areas.*

OF ALL SOUTHERN AFRICA'S natural systems, wetlands, in the widest sense of the word, have been the most impacted by man. Man's exploitation of wetlands is understandable and largely justified for water is the most essential single resource needed by the region's burgeoning human population. The utilization and management of the subcontinent's water resources has become a massive industry: the dams built to generate electricity and store water are among the largest in the world and the magnitude of basin transfer schemes, such as the Lesotho Highlands Water Project, almost defies the imagination. Every potential source of water for meeting projected demands is being looked at keenly: even such sacred natural systems as Okavango Delta, so far largely unscathed by man, have not escaped this calculated scrutiny. On a smaller scale, practically every catchment in the region has been subject to the manipulation of its water resource to some degree. In this process some aquatic systems have been winners and others losers, and the waterbirds associated with each have benefited or been victims accordingly.

As the numbers of people escalate, so the trend of exploiting, developing, redistributing and otherwise managing the region's water is likely to intensify and inflict further changes on the natural wetlands. There is good news and bad news in all this. The good news is for the species that can successfully exploit the spreading sea of storage dams over the region and can live with their unpredictable rapid draw-downs and often eutrophic condition. Species benefiting from this, such as the Redknobbed Coot and ducks and geese during their moult, have been mentioned. This chapter, however, targets the species for which all this and more is bad news – the species that are not living successfully with 20th-century water- and industrial-technology banging on their door.

In the 1960s the concept of Red Data books was first introduced as a means of identifying and ranking species at risk. These books list and rank the threatened species of a region using various population criteria of the species to determine the level of threat. Among the criteria to be answered are, for example: is the bird endemic to the region? Is its population declining? What is its numerical strength? What is its range? The Red Data books rank species into one of five threatened categories ranging from the most severe, 'extinct', through 'endangered', 'vulnerable' and 'rare' to the least threatened category, 'indeterminate'. Other categories outside this ranking are 'of special concern' and 'out of danger'. The only southern African country thus far to have produced a Red Data book on its birds is South Africa and one has also been compiled for the African continent as a whole. These two useful volumes provide the best current means of assessing which waterbird species are most at risk in southern Africa. The South African volume, last revised in 1984, lists 27 waterbirds at risk; one species is classed as extinct (African Skimmer), one as endangered (Wattled Crane), one as vulnerable (Bittern), 16 as rare (White Pelican, Pinkbacked Pelican, Rufousbellied Heron, Little Bittern, Woollynecked Stork, Openbilled Stork, Saddlebilled Stork, Yellowbilled Stork, Pygmy Goose, Whitewinged Flufftail, Lesser Jacana, Chestnutbanded Plover, Whitecrowned Plover, Redwinged Pratincole, Caspian Tern, Pel's Fishing Owl) and eight as indeterminate (Whitebacked Night Heron, Dwarf Bittern, Black Stork, Greater Flamingo, Lesser Flamingo, Baillon's Crake, African Finfoot, Grass Owl). On the other hand, the African Bird Red Data Book, published in 1985 by the International Council for Bird Preservation, ranks only two of these as threatened on a continental scale: Wattled Cranes are 'of special concern' and Whitewinged Flufftails are 'indeterminate'. Many of the species given Red Data status in South Africa are thus not considered threatened across the African continent as a whole. Not one waterbird species is endemic to

Where fish are superabundant, the co-operative fishing technique used by
White Pelicans breaks down and individuals tend to hunt solitarily (opposite).
The bird's expandable pouch is not for carrying or storing fish but serves as
a fish scoop. After each scoop the pelican tilts its head back to drain the water before
dipping again. Enormous wings enable these heavy-bodied birds to soar over the
great distances that may separate one lake from another (above).

*Seen against a winter landscape in the foothills of the Drakensberg, a stately
Wattled Crane stands aloof in its breeding marsh (above). These rare birds usually
nest in winter when the risk of damage from floods is minimal. Their nests,
which consist of large heaps of plant stems, are built in open ponds.*

South Africa; many that are found here range widely across Africa and some extend on to other continents as well. A number of the species given Red Data status in South Africa are not threatened in the sense that their numbers or range here have declined but because, being at the southern-most edge of their range, they nest here in small numbers and at few localities. The Redwinged Pratincole is such an example. Fewer than 100 pairs nest in South Africa where the species is 'rare', whereas elsewhere on the continent, and even in southern Africa (Mozambique and Botswana), breeding colonies numbering thousands of pairs are to be found. At least 10 other birds on the South African Red Data list reflect, to some extent, the same pattern. But, in making a meaningful assessment of the waterbird species at risk on the subcontinent, the South African list is a useful starting point. To this list must be added the Slaty Egret and Rock Pratincole, neither of which breeds in South Africa though both breed in small numbers and in restricted areas within the southern African limits.

Since rivers are unquestionably the most impacted of the aquatic systems in the region, the threatened bird species most reliant on these should be considered first. Water abstraction is but one of many impacts on the rivers and their birds. Damming floods and replaces the riverine habitat with open water, in some instances transforming only a few kilometres but in others – as is the case with Lake Kariba – hundreds of kilometres of river are lost. The dams act as sediment traps, and the larger the dam, the greater the trap. Thus the material that previously created the sandbars used as nest sites for some of the riverine species is no longer deposited downstream of the dams. In time, existing

The Woollynecked Stork (left), one of the least distinguished members of the stork family, is in appearance a rather dumpy, ungroomed bird which may be seen hanging around dirty-looking ponds along drying rivers. Generally uncommon throughout its African range, it centres its distribution in the subcontinent on the Okavango Delta. Like others of its family, it feeds on aquatic insects, crabs and frogs.

sandbars become vegetated so that nest sites for a few specialized species are not so readily available. In recent years, apparently as a result of this, African Skimmers have ceased breeding downstream of Lake Kariba and the numbers of Whitefronted Plovers, which also nest on the sandbars along the river, have been greatly diminished. African Skimmers also nest along the Kavango River in Caprivi and in northern Botswana, laying eggs between July and September when water levels are low and nests are unlikely to be flooded. Human disturbance at the nesting colonies here is increasing; some is deliberate as the chicks are sought for bait or food, some happens inadvertently when fishermen alight on a nesting island so preventing the birds from shielding the eggs and young from the harsh sun. There are reports of whole colonies losing all their eggs and young in this way. With the increasing human pressure along these rivers and little incentive to conserve the nesting colonies, these African Skimmers face a bleak future. Clearly, they are among the southern African waterbirds that are at risk.

Like the African Skimmer, Rock Pratincoles, which are also restricted to the Zambezi, Chobe, Kavango, and Kwando rivers, have suffered a reduction of their preferred habitat following the construction of Lake Kariba and Lake Cahora Bassa; if other proposed dams along the Zambezi materialize, both species will be further impacted. As their name suggests, Rock Pratincoles nest on rocky islands in the rivers and the sandbar problem does not affect them.

The Whitebacked Night Heron, Black Stork, Saddlebilled Stork, African Finfoot and Pel's Fishing Owl, which live along the larger, perennial rivers in southern Africa, are impacted to varying degrees by reduced water flow. Even before today's high levels of water abstraction from rivers, these birds had to cope with reduced flow resulting from droughts and in those circumstances some probably moved downstream to the estuaries and others concentrated at the remaining pools. But today's droughts have been compounded by water abstraction: some rivers now dry out completely during droughts and estuaries may become too saline to offer habitat to the affected species. There is thus an intuitive feeling that these species have declined in numbers and range over the region, although little by way of direct evidence exists in support of this supposition. For this reason, they have been accorded Red Data status in South Africa and the same threats facing them here are eventually likely to catch up with them elsewhere in Africa as well.

Disturbance of nesting birds is a factor inhibiting reproduction in other colonial ground-nesting species besides African Skimmers. Three species in particular, the White Pelican, Greater Flamingo and Lesser Flamingo, nest on the ground in large, conspicuous colonies and are very sensitive to disturbance. Lesser Flamingos, for example, nest at fewer than 10 places across the African continent, despite their large numbers (their total population is estimated to be two million birds) and their wide range which extends from west to east and southern Africa. Their chosen breeding sites are almost inaccessible to both man and predator and mass desertion of eggs has been recorded at colonies when they have been disturbed. The two southern African nesting sites, in the Etosha and Makgadikgadi pans, are typical of those used elsewhere in Africa where successful breeding can be achieved only when the pans are inundated with sufficient water to last the duration of the breeding cycle. Because of their sensitivity to disturbance and their vulnerability to predators, and because of the erratic availability of suitable conditions for breeding on these pans, these two flamingo species are at risk. Etosha Pan lies within a national park where human disturbance of the flamingo breeding colonies can be controlled but the Makgadikgadi site relies solely on its inaccessibility for protection. This

Characteristic of the African Openbill is its long, straight upper mandible which, with the lower one slightly upcurved, forms a gap near the end of the beak (opposite, above). This beak is supposedly designed for catching snails and mussels, items which are located while the bird wades slowly about in shallow water. When found, they are picked up by the tip of the beak (opposite, below); the sharp upper edge of the lower mandible cuts the mollusc from its shell which is discarded almost undamaged while its contents are swallowed. These distinctive storks come and go erratically in southern Africa, responding to periods of high and low rainfall and the establishment of freshwater mussel beds in the region's wetlands.

has diminished in recent years with the development of a multi-million rand soda ash project on the shores of the pan north-east of the colony and, while the development itself may not impact on the breeding flamingos, it has reduced the remoteness and inaccessibility of the area and made it more vulnerable to disturbance. Increased air traffic, a network of access roads, power lines and large numbers of people attracted to work at the factory all threaten successful breeding at this site in the years ahead.

White Pelicans face the same set of problems. Feeding conditions may be ideal but unless a safe breeding site is available they are unable to reproduce successfully. The largest recorded breeding colony, at which about 25 000 pairs commenced nesting on Lake Rukwa in Tanzania, failed when the water level receded and predators were able to reach the nests. At Lake Oponono in northern Namibia breeding was attempted in 1968, 1971 and 1980, but each time human disturbance led to desertion of the colonies. Islands off the south-western Cape coast, including Seal Island and Dyer Island, once provided White Pelicans with safe breeding sites but the build-up in seal numbers has

The Pinkbacked Pelican (below) is often mistaken for the more common White Pelican: it is, however, appreciably smaller and (in adults) greyer plumaged, and has a distinctive circular orbital ring around the eye. It differs in habits too: it fishes solitarily (not in flocks like the White Pelican), usually swimming close to the shore, and builds its nest in a tree, unlike the White Pelican, which nests on the ground.

forced the pelicans off. As a result, White Pelicans now nest regularly only on the protected islands in Lake St Lucia, on Dassen Island (another protected site off the west coast) and on the guano platform off Walvis Bay. Occasionally, when local conditions are favourable, they attempt to nest at other sites as they have done on Etosha Pan, Makgadikgadi and Lake Ngami.

Caspian Terns, which are also Red Data listed in South Africa, in many ways mirror the needs of the White Pelican: safe nesting sites within reach of good fishing waters. It is no coincidence that the islands of Lake St Lucia support the largest southern African breeding populations not only of the pelican but also of the Caspian Tern, and this is in no small measure the result of tight control on human access.

It is clear that waterbird conservation hinges on safeguarding waterbird habitats. In some species with generalized nesting habits, it may be foraging areas that are of critical importance; in others, such as the colonial breeding species, the availability of safe nesting sites may be the essential factor that dictates their occurrence. There are many waterbird species in which there is no dichotomy between breeding and foraging habitat: crakes and other Rallidae spend their lives in vleis of one or other kind, breeding, roosting, moulting and foraging in the same confined area. For these, as habitat is lost so a proportion of the population disappears. Two species that have been hard hit by loss of habitat are the Wattled Crane, sometimes ranked as South Africa's most endangered bird, and the Bittern. Both live in vleis, the crane restricted to permanent marshes in the upper reaches of river catchments and the Bittern found in both permanent and seasonal vleis and floodplains.

Wattled Cranes are large, conspicuous birds that are closely tied to wetlands. The type specimen of this species came from the south-western Cape where it (and the Bittern) formerly nested at Soetendalsvlei, near Bredasdorp. Today, however, both species have disappeared not only from here but from the Cape Province as a whole. The cranes are now confined (in South Africa) to upland marshes in the foothills of Natal's Drakensberg mountains and in the south-eastern Transvaal where they live as scattered pairs of which there are currently about one hundred. One by one the various vleis in which they nested have been rendered unsuitable: many have been drained, some have been inundated by dams, yet others have been engulfed by human activity which has prevented the birds from nesting successfully.

The South African Wattled Crane population is a small, isolated fragment of the species' entire African population which centres on Zambia. However, the fact that several thousand birds are estimated to be surviving in that country is no cause for complacency, for the massive range-reduction suffered by the South African population may be repeated elsewhere in Africa in the future. If there had been complacency about safeguarding the last surviving White Rhino population in South Africa at a time when thousands still occurred elsewhere on the continent, this animal would probably be extinct today. The small number of these animals that were protected in Natal eventually became the largest surviving population when large-scale poaching virtually eliminated the species elsewhere in Africa. And it was from Natal that White Rhinos were sent to recolonize those places from which they had disappeared.

Bitterns are far less conspicuous than Wattled Cranes and unless they are calling they are virtually undetectable. However, until the end of the first half of this century they were relatively frequently recorded and a dozen or more reports were made of nests, but since then records of the birds, and especially of nesting, have been rare.

A rare, secretive Whitebacked Night Heron (below) emerges from its daytime hide-out to fish along a river bank. Its large eyes, exaggerated by white eye-rings, facilitate night hunting. Little is known of this heron's fishing methods or, indeed, of its behaviour in general. The wispy white feathers responsible for its name are not readily apparent unless the bird is seen in flight.

With their upper and lower beak mandibles of
unequal length, African Skimmers (right and below)
are certainly odd-looking birds. This peculiar bill
structure is an adaptation to their unique foraging
technique: the birds catch fish just below the surface of
the water by flying with the beak opened and the
longer lower mandible cutting the water. When the
beak makes contact with prey, it snaps closed. Most
fishing is done at dusk and even after dark when it
seems shoals of small fish move close to the surface.
Sandbars exposed by low water levels are the focus of
skimmer activity: the birds roost on them during the
day, and nest on them, laying their clutch of speckled
eggs in a deep nest scrape (above).

The African Marsh Harrier (opposite) is closely tied to wetlands with emergent vegetation. Generally it hunts by sailing slowly above the grass or reed-tops, wings held stiffly in a shallow 'V', and flapping at intervals to prevent stalling (above, right). When prey is spotted the harrier drops to the ground, snatching the victim in its talons. These hawks take a wide range of prey, from birds (especially small finches living in the reeds) and rodents to frogs and insects. They also scavenge on occasions and feed on dead fish that have been washed up. Their graceful flight is countered by their nondescript plumage: speckled and barred in shades of brown and grey, they lack any distinctive plumage features by which they can be identified. The small, distinctly cowled head is a typical harrier character, however, and their marshland habitat is sufficient to separate them from other southern African species.

Many of their former haunts have been drained or reclaimed – a fate that befell the famous Potchefstroom marshes where the early ornithologist F. Barratt reported the bird to be 'found plentifully' in 1876, and those around Matatiele where Finch-Davies found three nests in the early 1900s. The species is ranked as 'vulnerable' in South Africa but on face value it may be threatened with extinction. It is apparently equally rare elsewhere in southern Africa: it has been recorded on a few occasions in Mozambique, only once (in the last century) in Botswana and never in Namibia or Zimbabwe.

The marsh habitats support several other secretive waterbirds. The Whitewinged Flufftail and Baillon's Crake are two that are Red Data listed and both are likely to have been affected by loss of habitat in the same way as the Bittern. As an example, one of the very few regular haunts of the flufftail, Franklin Marsh in East Griqualand, has been reduced in area from 2 500 hectares to its present size of 1 060 hectares as a result of agricultural encroachment and draining. On a larger scale, it has been estimated that 60 per cent of the vleis in the catchment of the Mfolozi River in Natal have been lost in recent times as a result of overgrazing or drainage. Overgrazing of upland marshes is particularly severe on the Grass Owl, another Red Data listed species that lives in rank vegetation along vleis.

The community of waterbird species dependent on seasonal floodplains is well served in southern Africa by the presence of the Okavango Delta and the wetlands in Caprivi. Thus a number of South African Red Data species, restricted in numbers and range in South Africa, are well represented in these wetlands: Pygmy Goose, Lesser Jacana and Dwarf Bittern are among them and are clearly not at risk on a subcontinental scale. Nor is the Slaty Egret at risk as long as the hydrological regime of the Delta, to which it is essentially restricted as a breeding bird, remains intact. In South Africa, however, much of the floodplain habitat is threatened with development of one kind or another.

The water that used to inundate the Pongolo floodplain is now trapped by Jozini Dam and although it is released to simulate natural flood events, this practice may well be jeopardized by developments in the future. Another vulnerable system is the Nyl floodplain which is gradually being strangled by the plethora of dams and by escalating water abstraction taking place in its catchment.

If southern Africa's natural wetlands and their spectacular array of waterbirds are to survive into the 21st century a greater balance needs to be sought between exploitation and conservation. True, there is a growing awareness of the biological value of wetlands and legislation now prevents developments from ploughing ahead irrespective of the consequences to the environment. For example, plans to exploit minerals within the Lake St Lucia wetland area have been put on hold pending the results of a detailed environmental impact assessment (EIA), and a scheme to dredge 45 kilometres of the Boro channel in the Okavango has been shelved as a result of the findings of the impact study. With the EIA procedure now routinely applied to developments such as these, the conservation lobby has an opportunity to scrutinize the assessments and enter the debate on the environmental costs and social benefits of such schemes. A second positive development is the formal international recognition given to wetlands by the Ramsar Convention. South Africa is so far its only signatory among the southern African countries; in 1991 there were 65 contracting countries to the Convention and 546 wetlands accorded international recognition. Twelve South African wetlands covering an area of 265 000 hectares are currently registered as Ramsar sites: they include Lake St Lucia, Langebaan Lagoon, Barberspan, De Hoop estuary, and others. In South Africa there is also legislation aimed at safeguarding wetlands; for example, sponge areas may not be drained nor may effluent be discharged into rivers. Another positive development in this country is that the biotic community is now taken into account when allocating water, a situation that did not exist a decade ago. To this end research is being conducted to establish the water requirements of the biota dependent on the rivers flowing through the Kruger National Park, so that a portion of this limited resource also reaches them.

Wetland conservation rests not just with the legislators, water authorities and big-time developers: municipalities, local communities, landowners and ordinary people can all take positive steps in promoting it. Enhancing the awareness and respect of these vital areas by ordinary people is the most effective way of achieving this end and, because the waterbirds themselves are the wetlands' most colourful and conspicuous ambassadors, they are the lure to attract both appreciation by and the support of the people of southern Africa.

Enormous, sharp-toed feet and large, black eyes are the secretive Pel's Fishing Owl's main tools for survival (opposite). These rare birds hunt nocturnally and live on fish which they catch from perches overhanging the water. Since their prey is under water, silent flight, usual in other owl species, is unnecessary and Pel's Fishing Owls fly with a noisy whooshing flapping. During the day they hide in thickly foliaged trees and are consequently seldom seen.

WETLANDS; REGION; SIZE	CONSERVATION STATUS**	KEY SPECIES
RIVERS*		
Kavango, Namibia and Botswana (11 750 000)		Rock Pratincole, African Skimmer
Orange-Vaal, South Africa (12 057 000)		Goliath Heron, Whitebacked Night Heron
Zambezi, Zimbabwe and Mozambique (88 000 000)		Rock Pratincole, African Skimmer, Whitebacked Night Heron, Whitefronted Plover, Whitecrowned Plover
MARSHES		
Blesbokspruit, South Africa (<1 000 ha)	R; 20%=PNR	herons, crakes, waders
Blood River, South Africa (<1 000 ha)		crakes
Franklin Marsh, South Africa (1 000 ha)		crakes
Klipspruit, South Africa (<1 000 ha)		herons, crakes, waders
Lakenvlei, South Africa (<1 000 ha)		cranes, crakes
Memelvlei, South Africa (1 800 ha)		cranes
Natalspruit, South Africa (<1 000 ha)		herons, crakes, waders
Wakkerstroom Marsh, South Africa (<1 000 ha)		cranes, crakes
FLOODPLAINS		
Chobe-Linyanti, Namibia (20 000 ha)		Longtoed Plover, Redwinged Pratincole, Openbilled Stork
Inkomati, Mozambique (>1 000 ha)		Redwinged Pratincole
Mkuze, South Africa (18 000 ha)	70%=PNR	herons, crakes, ducks, Pinkbacked Pelican, Yellowbilled Stork
Nyl, South Africa (16 000 ha)	10%=PNR	herons, crakes, ducks
Okavango, Botswana (1 500 000 ha)	20%=GR	Slaty Egret, Pel's Fishing Owl, Pygmy Goose
Pongolo, South Africa (12 000 ha)	10%=PNR	ducks
Pungwe River, Mozambique (>1 000 ha)		ducks, storks
PANS		
Barberspan, South Africa (2 000 ha)	R; 100%=PNR	flamingos, ducks (moulting), coots
Bushmanland Panveld, Namibia		ducks, flamingos, Openbilled Stork, Slaty Egret
Chrissie, South Africa (1 000 ha)		flamingos, waders
Etosha, Namibia (820 000 ha)	100%=NP	flamingos, White Pelican
Hwange Panveld, Zimbabwe	100%=NP	crakes, ducks
Makgadikgadi, Botswana (1 000 000 ha)	10%=GR	flamingos, White Pelican, waders, Chestnutbanded Plover
Ngami, Botswana (20 000 ha)		ducks, waders, Redwinged Pratincole, Greater Flamingo, White Pelican
Rietvlei, South Africa (<1 000 ha)		ducks, coots, waders
Vanwyk's vlei, South Africa (680 ha)		Greater Flamingo
Welkom Pans, South Africa (<1 000 ha)		flamingos, S A Shelduck

WETLANDS; REGION; SIZE	CONSERVATION STATUS**	KEY SPECIES
IMPOUNDMENTS		
Bloemhof, South Africa (23 000 ha)	80%=PNR	Goliath Heron, waders
Cahora Bassa, Mozambique (274 000 ha)		ducks, herons, storks
Jozini, South Africa (13 000 ha)	70%=PNR	Pinkbacked Pelican, Yellowbilled Stork
Kariba, Zimbabwe (440 000 ha)		African Fish Eagle
Kyle, Zimbabwe (9 100 ha)	100%=NP	cormorants, Darter
PK le Roux, South Africa (14 000 ha)		cormorants
Robertson, Zimbabwe (8 100 ha)		ducks, waders
Vaal, South Africa (29 000 ha)	10%=PNR	waders
Verwoerd, South Africa (36 000 ha)		ducks, cormorants
LAKES		
Bambene, Mozambique (<1 000 ha)		flamingos
Chuali, Mozambique (<1 000 ha)		ducks (esp. Fulvous Duck, Southern Pochard)
Kosi Bay, South Africa	R; PNR	Pel's Fishing Owl
Liambezi, Namibia (10 000 ha)		Pinkbacked Pelican, storks, ducks
St Lucia, South Africa (32 000 ha)	R; 100%=PNR	Greater Flamingo, Caspian Tern, White Pelican, waders, herons
Sibayi, South Africa (6 500 ha)	R	ducks
Wilderness-Sedgefield Lakes, South Africa (850 ha)	R	ducks, coots, Osprey
ESTUARIES		
Berg, South Africa (800 ha)		waders, flamingos
De Hoop Vlei, South Africa (750 ha)	R; 100%=PNR	White Pelican, Greater Flamingo, coots
Kunene, Namibia (<1 000 ha)		waders, terns, flamingos, White Pelican
Orange River mouth, South Africa (2 000 ha)	R	cormorants, gulls, waders, flamingos
Richard's Bay, South Africa (<1 000 ha)		waders, flamingos
Sandwich Harbour, Namibia (2 800 ha)		waders, flamingos
Swartkops, South Africa (<1 000 ha)		waders (esp. Whimbrel), terns, gulls, flamingos
Zambezi Delta, Mozambique (>1 000 ha)		Wattled Crane, storks, ducks
LAGOONS		
Langebaan, South Africa (6 000 ha)	R; 100%=NP	waders, flamingos
Walvis Bay, South Africa (>1 000 ha)		waders, flamingos

*Rivers measured in million cubic metres mean annual run-off

**R = Ramsar site
PNR = Provincial Nature Reserve
NP = National Park
GR = Game Reserve

MAJOR WETLAND AREAS IN SOUTHERN AFRICA

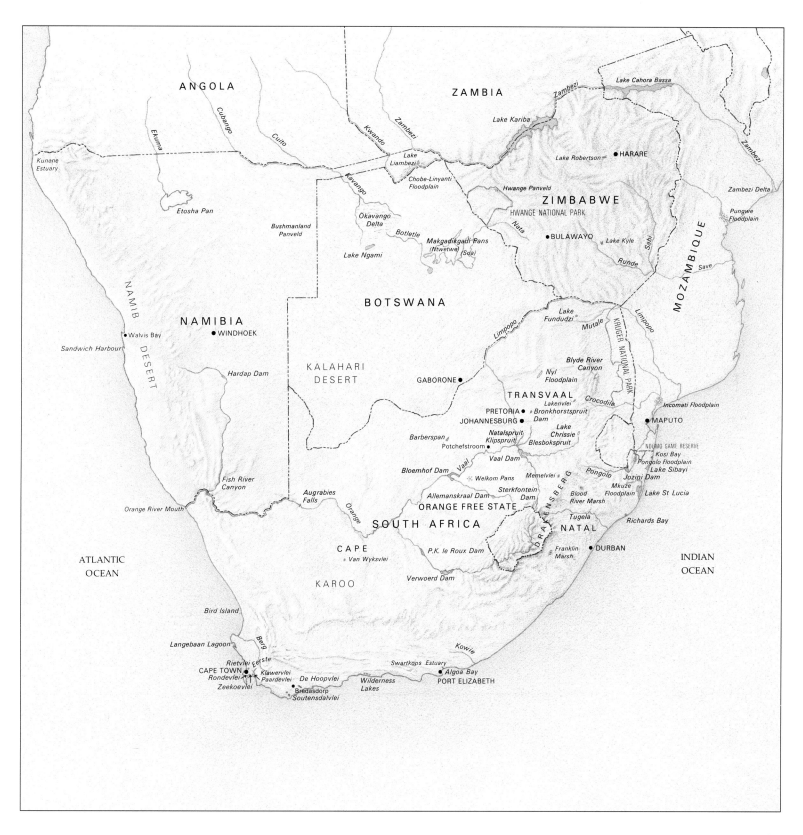

FAMILY	SPECIES AND SCIENTIFIC NAME	APPROX WEIGHT	WORLD BREEDING RANGE	SOUTHERN AFRICAN STATUS AND RELATIVE ABUNDANCE	RED DATA STATUS IN SOUTHERN AFRICA	PREFERRED HABITAT IN SOUTHERN AFRICA
GREBE	Great Crested Grebe *Podiceps cristatus*	600g	Africa, Eurasia, Australasia	breeding resident; locally common	nil	open water
	Blacknecked Grebe *Podiceps nigricollis*	300g	Africa, Eurasia, N America	breeding resident; locally common	nil	open water
	Dabchick *Tachybaptus ruficollis*	150g	Africa, Eurasia	breeding resident; abundant	nil	open water
PELICAN	White Pelican *Pelecanus onocrotalus*	7,5kg	Africa, Eurasia	breeding resident; scarce	'rare'	open water
	Pinkbacked Pelican *Pelecanus rufescens*	5kg	Africa	breeding resident; scarce	'rare'	open water
CORMORANT	Whitebreasted Cormorant *Phalacrocorax carbo*	1,6kg	Africa, Eurasia, Australasia, N America	breeding resident; common	nil	open water, rivers
	Reed Cormorant *Phalacrocorax africanus*	500g	Africa	breeding resident; common	nil	open water, rivers
DARTER	Darter *Anhinga melanogaster*	1,5kg	Africa, Asia, Australia	breeding resident; common	nil	open water
HERON	Grey Heron *Ardea cinerea*	1,5kg	Africa, Eurasia	breeding resident; common	nil	open water, marshes, rivers
EGRET	Goliath Heron *Ardea goliath*	4,3kg	Africa, Middle East	breeding resident; scarce	nil	open water, marshes, rivers
BITTERN	Purple Heron *Ardea purpurea*	900g	Africa, Eurasia	breeding resident; common	nil	marshes
	Great White Egret *Egretta alba*	1,1kg	Africa, Eurasia, Australasia, Americas	breeding resident; common	nil	open water, marshes, rivers
	Little Egret *Egretta garzetta*	350g	Africa, Eurasia, Australasia	breeding resident; common	nil	open water, rivers
	Yellowbilled Egret *Egretta intermedia*	400g	Africa, Asia, Australia	breeding resident; fairly common	nil	open water, marshes
	Black Egret *Egretta ardesiaca*	310g	Africa	breeding resident; scarce	nil	open water, marshes
	Slaty Egret *Egretta vinaceigula*	300g	south-central Africa	breeding resident; scarce	nil	open water, marshes
	Little Blue Heron *Egretta caerulea*	350g	Americas	non-breeding vagrant; rare	nil	open water
	Squacco Heron *Ardeola ralloides*	300g	Africa, Europe	breeding resident; fairly common	nil	marshes
	Malagassy Squacco Heron *Ardeola idae*	300g	Madagascar, East Africa	non-breeding vagrant; rare	nil	marshes
	Greenbacked Heron *Butorides striatus*	200g	Africa, Asia, Australasia, Americas	breeding resident; common	nil	rivers
	Rufousbellied Heron *Ardeola rufiventris*	n/a	south-central Africa	breeding visitor; scarce	'rare'	marshes
	Blackcrowned Night Heron *Nycticorax nycticorax*	500g	Africa, Eurasia, Americas	breeding resident; fairly common	nil	marshes, open water
	Whitebacked Night Heron *Gorsachius leuconotus*	440g	Africa	breeding resident; scarce	'indeterminate'	river
	Little Bittern *Ixobrychus minutus*	100g	Africa, Eurasia, Australia	breeding resident; scarce	'rare'	marshes
	Dwarf Bittern *Ixobrychus sturmii*	140g	Africa	breeding visitor; scarce	'indeterminate'	marshes
	Bittern *Botaurus stellaris*	1kg	Africa, Eurasia	breeding resident; rare	'vulnerable'	marshes
HAMERKOP	Hamerkop *Scopus umbretta*	420g	Africa	breeding resident; common	nil	rivers, marshes, open water
STORK	Black Stork *Ciconia nigra*	3kg	Africa, Eurasia	breeding resident; scarce	'indeterminate'	rivers, open water
	Woollynecked Stork *Ciconia episcopus*	n/a	Africa, Asia	breeding resident; scarce	'rare'	rivers, marshes
	Openbilled Stork *Anastomus lamelligerus*	1,2kg	Africa	breeding resident; scarce	'rare'	rivers, marshes
	Saddlebilled Stork *Ephippiorhynchus senegalensis*	6kg	Africa	breeding resident; scarce	'rare'	rivers, marshes
	Yellowbilled Stork *Mycteria ibis*	2,5kg	Africa	breeding resident; locally common	'rare'	open water, marshes
IBIS	Sacred Ibis *Threskiornis aethiopicus*	1,3kg	Africa	breeding resident; common	nil	open water, marshes
SPOONBILL	Glossy Ibis *Plegadis falcinellus*	520g	Africa, Eurasia, Australasia, Americas	breeding resident; common	nil	open water, marshes
	African Spoonbill *Platalea alba*	1,8kg	Africa	breeding resident; common	nil	open water, marshes
FLAMINGO	Greater Flamingo *Phoenicopterus ruber*	2,5kg	Africa, Eurasia, central America	breeding resident; locally abundant	'indeterminate'	open water
	Lesser Flamingo *Phoenicopterus minor*	1,7kg	Africa, Middle East	breeding resident; locally abundant	'indeterminate'	open water
SWAN	Mute Swan *Cygnus olor*	10kg	Eurasia, introd. in South Africa	feral; has bred; extinct?	nil	open water
DUCK	Whitefaced Duck *Dendrocygna viduata*	740g	Africa, South America	breeding resident; common	nil	open water, marshes
GOOSE	Fulvous Duck *Dendrocygna bicolor*	700g	Africa, Asia, Americas	breeding resident; fairly common	nil	open water, marshes

FAMILY	SPECIES AND SCIENTIFIC NAME	APPROX WEIGHT	WORLD BREEDING RANGE	SOUTHERN AFRICAN STATUS AND RELATIVE ABUNDANCE	RED DATA STATUS IN SOUTHERN AFRICA	PREFERRED HABITAT IN SOUTHERN AFRICA
SWAN DUCK GOOSE	Whitebacked Duck *Thalassornis leuconotus*	680g	Africa	breeding resident; fairly common	nil	open water, marshes
	Egyptian Goose *Alopochen aegyptiacus*	2kg	Africa	breeding resident; abundant	nil	open water, marshes, rivers
	South African Shelduck *Tadorna cana*	1,2kg	Southern Africa	breeding resident; common	nil	open water
	Yellowbilled Duck *Anas undulata*	900g	Africa	breeding resident; common	nil	open water, marshes
	Mallard *Anas platyrhynchos*	1,1kg	Eurasia, North America; introd. S Africa	feral; breeds; localized	nil	open water
	African Black Duck *Anas sparsa*	900g	Africa	breeding resident; fairly common	nil	rivers
	Cape Teal *Anas capensis*	400g	Africa	breeding resident; common	nil	open shores
	Hottentot Teal *Anas hottentota*	240g	Africa	breeding resident; fairly common	nil	open water, marshes
	Redbilled Teal *Anas erythrorhyncha*	550g	Africa	breeding resident; common	nil	open water, marshes
	Pintail *Anas acuta*	700g	Eurasia, North America	non-breeding vagrant; rare	nil	open water
	Garganey *Anas querquedula*	340g	Eurasia	non-breeding vagrant; rare	nil	open water
	European Shoveller *Anas clypeata*	600g	Eurasia, North America	non-breeding vagrant; rare	nil	open water
	Cape Shoveller *Anas smithii*	650g	Southern Africa	breeding resident; common	nil	open water
	Southern Pochard *Netta erythrophthalma*	780g	Africa, South Africa	breeding resident; common	nil	open water, marshes
	Pygmy Goose *Nettapus auritus*	280g	Africa	breeding resident; scarce	'rare'	open water, marshes
	Knobbilled Duck *Sarkidiornis melanotos*	1,7kg	Africa, Asia, South America	breeding resident; fairly common	nil	open water, marshes
	Spurwinged Goose *Plectropterus gambensis*	6kg	Africa	breeding resident; common	nil	open water, marshes
	Maccoa Duck *Oxyura maccoa*	600g	Africa	breeding resident; scarce	nil	open water
BIRDS OF PREY	African Fish Eagle *Haliaeetus vocifer*	3kg	Africa	breeding resident; locally common	nil	open water, rivers
	European Marsh Harrier *Circus aeruginosus*	600g	Eurasia	non-breeding visitor; rare	nil	marshes
	African Marsh Harrier *Circus ranivorus*	500g	Africa	breeding resident; scarce	nil	marshes
	Osprey *Pandion haliaetus*	1,5kg	Africa, Eurasia, Australasia, Americas	non-breeding visitor; scarce	nil	open water
CRANE	Wattled Crane *Grus carunculatus*	7kg	Africa	breeding resident; scarce	'endangered'	marshes
	Crowned Crane *Balearica regulorum*	3,6kg	Africa	breeding resident; fairly common	nil	marshes
RAIL CRAKE FLUFFTAIL MOORHEN GALLINULE	African Rail *Rallus caerulescens*	160g	Africa	breeding resident; common	nil	marshes
	African Crake *Crex egregia*	130g	Africa	breeding visitor; scarce	nil	marshes
	Black Crake *Amaurornis flavirostris*	90g	Africa	breeding resident; common	nil	marshes, rivers
	Spotted Crake *Porzana porzana*	70g	Europe	non-breeding visitor; scarce	nil	marshes
	Baillon's Crake *Porzana pusilla*	30g	Africa, Eurasia, Australasia	breeding resident; scarce	'indeterminate'	marshes
	Striped Crake *Aenigmatolimnas marginalis*	60g	Africa	breeding visitor; scarce	nil	marshes
	Redchested Flufftail *Sarothrura rufa*	35g	Africa	breeding resident; common	nil	marshes
	Streakybreasted Flufftail *Sarothrura boehmi*	n/a	Africa	breeding visitor; scarce	nil	marshes
	Whitewinged Flufftail *Sarothrura ayresi*	35g	Africa	breeding visitor?; rare	'rare'	marshes
	Purple Gallinule *Porphyrio porphyrio*	550g	Africa, Eurasia, Australasia, Americas	breeding resident; common	nil	marshes
	Lesser Gallinule *Porphyrula alleni*	160g	Africa	breeding visitor; scarce	nil	marshes
	American Purple Gallinule *Porphyrula martinica*	230g	Americas	non-breeding vagrant; rare	nil	marshes
	Moorhen *Gallinula chloropus*	250g	Africa, Eurasia, Americas	breeding resident; abundant	nil	marshes, open water
	Lesser Moorhen *Gallinula angulata*	160g	Africa	breeding visitor; locally common	nil	marshes
	Redknobbed Coot *Fulica cristata*	750g	Africa, S Europe	breeding resident; abundant	nil	open water
FINFOOT	African Finfoot *Podica senegalensis*	600g	Africa	breeding resident; scarce	'indeterminate'	rivers
JACANA	African Jacana *Actophilornis africanus*	180g	Africa	breeding resident; locally common	nil	marshes
	Lesser Jacana *Microparra capensis*	40g	Africa	breeding resident; scarce	'rare'	marshes
PAINTED SNIPE	Painted Snipe *Rostratula benghalensis*	120g	Africa, Asia, Australia	breeding resident; scarce	nil	marshes
PLOVER	Ringed Plover *Charadrius hiaticula*	60g	Eurasia, N America	non-breeding visitor; locally common	nil	open shores
	Whitefronted Plover *Charadrius marginatus*	50g	Africa	breeding resident; common	nil	open shores, rivers

FAMILY	SPECIES AND SCIENTIFIC NAME	APPROX WEIGHT	WORLD BREEDING RANGE	SOUTHERN AFRICAN STATUS AND RELATIVE ABUNDANCE	RED DATA STATUS IN SOUTHERN AFRICA	PREFERRED HABITAT IN SOUTHERN AFRICA
PLOVER	Chestnutbanded Plover *Charadrius pallidus*	35g	Africa	breeding resident; scarce	'rare'	open shores
	Kittlitz's Plover *Charadrius pecuarius*	40g	Africa	breeding resident; common	nil	open shores
	Threebanded Plover *Charadrius tricollaris*	30g	Africa	breeding resident; common	nil	open shores, rivers
	Mongolian Plover *Charadrius mongolus*	60g	Asia	non-breeding vagrant; rare	nil	open shores
	Greater Sandplover *Charadrius leschenaultii*	110g	Asia	non-breeding vagrant; rare	nil	open shores
	American Golden Plover *Pluvialis dominica*	120g	N America	non-breeding vagrant; rare	nil	open shores
	Pacific Golden Plover *Pluvialis fulva*	120g	N America	non-breeding vagrant; rare	nil	open shores
	Grey Plover *Pluvialis squatarola*	230g	Asia, N America	non-breeding visitor; locally common	nil	open shores
	Blacksmith Plover *Vanellus armatus*	150g	Africa	breeding resident; abundant	nil	open shores, marshes
	Whitecrowned Plover *Vanellus albiceps*	180g	Africa	breeding resident; scarce	'rare'	rivers
	Wattled Plover *Vanellus senegallus*	220g	Africa	breeding resident; common	nil	marshes
	Longtoed Plover *Vanellus crassirostris*	190g	Africa	breeding resident; scarce	nil	marshes
SCOLOPACIDS	Turnstone *Arenaria interpres*	100g	Eurasia, N America	non-breeding visitor; locally common	nil	open shores
	Terek Sandpiper *Xenus cinereus*	70g	Eurasia	non-breeding visitor; scarce	nil	open shores
	Common Sandpiper *Tringa hypoleucos*	45g	Eurasia	non-breeding visitor; common	nil	open shores
	Green Sandpiper *Tringa ochropus*	80g	Eurasia	non-breeding visitor; scarce	nil	rivers
	Wood Sandpiper *Tringa glareola*	60g	Eurasia	non-breeding visitor; abundant	nil	open shores, marshes, rivers
	Spotted Redshank *Tringa erythropus*	170g	Eurasia	non-breeding vagrant; rare	nil	open shores
	Redshank *Tringa totanus*	130g	Eurasia	non-breeding vagrant; rare	nil	open shores
	Marsh Sandpiper *Tringa stagnatilis*	60g	Eurasia	non-breeding visitor; common	nil	open shores
	Greenshank *Tringa nebularia*	250g	Eurasia	non-breeding visitor; common	nil	open shores
	Greater Yellowlegs *Tringa melanoleuca*	160g	N America	non-breeding vagrant; rare	nil	open shores
	Lesser Yellowlegs *Tringa flavipes*	80g	N America	non-breeding vagrant; rare	nil	open shores
	Knot *Calidris canutus*	170g	Asia	non-breeding visitor; scarce	nil	open shores
	Curlew Sandpiper *Calidris ferruginea*	60g	Asia	non-breeding visitor; abundant	nil	open shores
	Dunlin *Calidris alpina*	45g	Eurasia, N America	non-breeding vagrant; rare	nil	open shores
	Little Stint *Calidris minuta*	25g	Eurasia	non-breeding visitor; abundant	nil	open shores
	Longtoed Stint *Calidris subminuta*	30g	Asia	non-breeding vagrant; rare	nil	open shores
	Rednecked Stint *Calidris ruficollis*	35g	Asia, N America	non-breeding vagrant; rare	nil	open shores
	Whiterumped Sandpiper *Calidris fuscicollis*	40g	N America	non-breeding vagrant; rare	nil	open shores
	Baird's Sandpiper *Calidris bairdii*	40g	N America	non-breeding vagrant; rare	nil	open shores
	Pectoral Sandpiper *Calidris melanotos*	100g	Asia, N America	non-breeding vagrant; rare	nil	open shores
	Temminck's Stint *Calidris temminckii*	20g	Eurasia	non-breeding vagrant; rare	nil	open shores
	Sanderling *Calidris alba*	75g	Asia, N America	non-breeding visitor; common	nil	open shores
	Buffbreasted Sandpiper *Tryngites subruficollis*	60g	N America	non-breeding vagrant; rare	nil	open shores
	Broadbilled Sandpiper *Limicola falcinellus*	40g	Eurasia	non-breeding vagrant; rare	nil	open shores
	Ruff *Phylomachus pugnax*	180g	Eurasia	non-breeding visitor; abundant	nil	open shores, marshes
	Great Snipe *Gallinago media*	200g	Eurasia	non-breeding vagrant; rare	nil	marshes
	Ethiopian Snipe *Gallinago nigripennis*	110g	Africa	breeding resident; common	nil	marshes
	Blacktailed Godwit *Limosa limosa*	420g	Eurasia	non-breeding vagrant; rare	nil	open shores
	Bartailed Godwit *Limosa lapponica*	340g	Eurasia, N America	non-breeding visitor; scarce	nil	open shores
	Hudsonian Godwit *Limosa haemastica*	n/a	N America	non-breeding vagrant; rare	nil	open shores
	Curlew *Numenius arquata*	700g	Eurasia	non-breeding visitor; scarce	nil	open shores
	Whimbrel *Numenius phaeopus*	420g	Eurasia	non-breeding visitor; locally common	nil	open shores
	Grey Phalarope *Phalaropus fulicarius*	55g	Eurasia, N America	non-breeding vagrant; rare	nil	open water
	Rednecked Phalarope *Phalaropus lobatus*	35g	Eurasia, N America	non-breeding vagrant; rare	nil	open water
	Wilson's Phalarope *Phalaropus tricolor*	55g	N America	non-breeding vagrant; rare	nil	open water
AVOCET	Avocet *Recurvirostra avosetta*	320g	Africa, Eurasia	breeding resident; common	nil	open water
STILT	Blackwinged Stilt *Himantopus himantopus*	180g	Africa, Eurasia, Australasia, Americas	breeding resident; common	nil	open water, marshes

FAMILY	SPECIES AND SCIENTIFIC NAME	APPROX WEIGHT	WORLD BREEDING RANGE	SOUTHERN AFRICAN STATUS AND RELATIVE ABUNDANCE	RED DATA STATUS IN SOUTHERN AFRICA	PREFERRED HABITAT IN SOUTHERN AFRICA
DIKKOP	Water Dikkop *Burhinus vermiculatus*	300g	Africa	breeding resident; common	nil	rivers
PRATINCOLE	Redwinged Pratincole *Glareola pratincola*	80g	Africa, Eurasia	breeding visitor; locally common	'rare'	open shores, rivers, marshes
	Rock Pratincole *Glareola nuchalis*	50g	Africa	breeding visitor; scarce	nil	rivers
GULL	Lesser Blackbacked Gull *Larus fuscus*	750g	Eurasia	non-breeding vagrant; rare	nil	open water
TERN	Greyheaded Gull *Larus cirrocephalus*	280g	Africa, S America	breeding resident; common	nil	open water
	Franklin's Gull *Larus pipixcan*	280g	N America	non-breeding vagrant; rare	nil	open water
	Blackheaded Gull *Larus ridibundus*	250g	Eurasia	non-breeding vagrant; rare	nil	open water
	Gullbilled Tern *Gelochelidon nilotica*	190g	N Africa, Eurasia, Australia, Americas	non-breeding vagrant; rare	nil	open water
	Caspian Tern *Hydroprogne caspia*	630g	Africa, Eurasia, Australasia, N America	breeding resident; scarce	'rare'	open water
	Black Tern *Chlidonias niger*	70g	Eurasia, N America	non-breeding vagrant; rare	nil	open water
	Whiskered Tern *Chlidonias hybridus*	65g	Africa, Eurasia, Australia	breeding resident; fairly common	nil	open water, marshes
	Whitewinged Tern *Chlidonias leucopterus*	60g	Eurasia	non-breeding visitor; common	nil	open water, marshes
SKIMMER	African Skimmer *Rynchops flavirostris*	160g	Africa	breeding visitor; scarce	'extinct'	rivers
OWL	Grass Owl *Tyto capensis*	420g	Africa	breeding resident; scarce	'indeterminate'	marshes
	Marsh Owl *Asio capensis*	320g	Africa	breeding resident; common	nil	marshes
	Pel's Fishing Owl *Scotopelia peli*	2,2kg	Africa	breeding resident; scarce	'rare'	rivers
KINGFISHER	Pied Kingfisher *Ceryle rudis*	80g	Africa, Eurasia	breeding resident; common	nil	rivers, open water
	Giant Kingfisher *Ceryle maxima*	350g	Africa	breeding resident; fairly common	nil	rivers, open water
	Halfcollared Kingfisher *Alcedo semitorquata*	40g	Africa	breeding resident; fairly common	nil	rivers
	Malachite Kingfisher *Alcedo cristata*	20g	Africa	breeding resident; common	nil	rivers, open water
SWALLOW	Brownthroated Martin *Riparia paludicola*	14g	Africa, Asia	breeding resident; common	nil	rivers, open water
WARBLER	European Reed Warbler *Acrocephalus scirpaceus*	11g	Eurasia	non-breeding vagrant; rare	nil	marshes
	African Marsh Warbler *Acrocephalus baeticatus*	11g	Africa	breeding visitor; common	nil	marshes
	Cinnamon Reed Warbler *Acrocephalus cinnamomeus*	11g	Africa	non-breeding vagrant; rare	nil	marshes
	European Marsh Warbler *Acrocephalus palustris*	13g	Eurasia	non-breeding visitor; common	nil	marshes
	European Sedge Warbler *Acrocephalus schoenobaenus*	12g	Eurasia	non-breeding visitor; fairly common	nil	marshes
	Cape Reed Warbler *Acrocephalus gracilirostris*	19g	Africa	breeding resident; common	nil	marshes
	Greater Swamp Warbler *Acrocephalus rufescens*	n/a	Africa	breeding resident; locally common	nil	marshes
	African Sedge Warbler *Bradypterus baboecala*	15g	Africa	breeding resident; common	nil	marshes
	Blackbacked Cisticola *Cisticola galactotes*	13g	Africa	breeding resident; common	nil	marshes
	Chirping Cisticola *Cisticola pipiens*	16g	Africa	breeding resident; common	nil	marshes
	Levaillant's Cisticola *Cisticola tinniens*	13g	Africa	breeding resident; common	nil	marshes
WAGTAIL	African Pied Wagtail *Motacilla aguimp*	27g	Africa	breeding resident; common	nil	rivers, open shores
	Longtailed Wagtail *Motacilla clara*	19g	Africa	breeding resident; fairly common	nil	rivers
	Cape Wagtail *Motacilla capensis*	21g	Africa	breeding resident; abundant	nil	rivers, open shores
	Grey Wagtail *Motacilla cinerea*	18g	N Africa	non-breeding vagrant; rare	nil	rivers

FURTHER READING

ALLANSON, B. R., HART, R. C., O'KEEFFE, J. H. & ROBARTS, R. D. 1991. *Inland waters of southern Africa: an ecological perspective.* Kluwer, Dordrecht.

ARKELL, G. B. F. 1979. 'Aspects of the feeding and breeding habits of the Giant Kingfisher.' *Ostrich* 50:176-181.

BALL, I. J., FROST, P. G. H., SIEGFRIED, W. R. & MCKINNEY, F. M. 1978. 'Territories and local movements of African Black Ducks.' *Wildfowl* 29:61-79.

BEGG, G. 1986. *The Wetlands of Natal.* Town & Regional Planning Commission, Pietermaritzburg.

BERRUTI, A. 1983. 'The biomass, energy consumption and breeding of waterbirds at Lake St Lucia.' *Ostrich* 54:65-82.

BERRY, H. H. 1972. 'Flamingo breeding on the Etosha Pan, South West Africa, during 1971.' *Madoqua Ser.* 1, 5:5-27.

BIRKHEAD, M. E. 1978. 'Some aspects of the feeding ecology of the Reed Cormorant and Darter on Lake Kariba, Rhodesia.' *Ostrich* 49:1-7.

BLAKE, D. 1969. 'The behaviour of *Egretta garzetta* and *E. intermedia.*' *Ostrich* 40:150-155.

BROOKE, R. K. 1984. *South African Red Data Book – Birds.* S. Afr. Natnl. Sci. Progr. Report no. 97.

BROWN, L. H. 1959. *The mystery of the flamingos.* Country Life, London.

BROWN, L. H. 1980. *The African Fish Eagle.* Bailey Bros & Swinfen, Folkstone.

BROWN, L. H. & URBAN, E. 1969. 'The breeding biology of the Great White Pelican *Pelecanus onocrotalus roseus* in Ethiopia.' *Ibis* 111:199-237.

CAMBRAY, J. A. 1985. 'Observations on the number of piscivorous birds below the P. K. le Roux Dam Wall, Orange River.' *Ostrich* 56:202-204.

CAMPBELL, A. C. 1976. 'Proceedings of the symposium on the Okavango Delta and its future utilisation.' Botswana Society, Gaborone.

COOPER, J., BROOKE, R. K., CYRUS, D. P., MARTIN, A. P., TAYLOR, R. H. & WILLIAMS, A. J. 1992. 'Distribution, population size and conservation of the Caspian Tern *Sterna caspia* in southern Africa.' *Ostrich* 63:58-67.

COPPINGER, M. P., WILLIAMS, G. D. & MACLEAN, G. L. 1988. 'Distribution and breeding biology of the African Skimmer on the upper and middle Zambezi River.' *Ostrich* 59:85-96.

DAVIES, B. R. & DAY, J. H. 1986. 'The biology and conservation of South Africa's vanishing waters.' Centre for Extramural Studies, University of Cape Town.

DAY, J. H. (ED.) 1981. *Estuarine ecology with particular reference to southern Africa.* Balkema, Cape Town.

DEPARTMENT OF WATER AFFAIRS. 1986. 'Management of the water resources of the Republic of South Africa.' Department of Water Affairs, Pretoria.

FERRAR, A. A. (ED.) 1989. 'Ecological flow requirements for South African rivers.' *South African National Scientific Programmes Report no.* 162.

FRASER, W. 1971. 'Birds at Lake Ngami, Botswana.' *Ostrich* 42:128-130.

GELDENHUYS, J. N. 1981. 'Breeding ecology of the South African Shelduck.' *South African Journal of Wildlife Research* 10.

GELDENHUYS, J. N. 1981. 'Moults and moult localities of the South African Shelduck.' *Ostrich* 52:129-134.

GUILLET, A. 1979. 'Aspects of the foraging behaviour of the Shoebill.' *Ostrich* 50:252-255.

HALE, W. G. 1980. *Waders.* Collins, London.

HANCOCK, J. & KUSHLAN, J. 1984. *The Herons Handbook.* Croom Helm, London.

HARWIN, R. M. 1984. 'Notes on the ecology of southern African Kingfishers.' Proceedings of the 5th Pan-African Ornithological Congress: 387-394.

HAYMAN, P., MARCHANT, J. & PRATER, T. 1986. *Shorebirds. An identification guide to the waders of the world.* Croom Helm, London.

HINES, C. 1989. 'The birds of north-eastern Namibia.' *Birding SA* 41:89-992.

HOPKINSON, G. & MASTERSON, A. 1984. 'The occurrence and ecological preferences of certain Rallidae near Salisbury, Zimbabwe.' Proceedings of the 5th Pan-African Ornithological Congress: 425-440.

JOHNSGARD, P. A. 1981. *The plovers, sandpipers and snipes of the world.* University of Nebraska Press, London.

JONES, P. J. 1978. 'A possible function of the "wing-drying" posture in the Reed Cormorant *Phalacrocorax africanus.*' *Ibis* 120:540-542.

KAHL, M. P. 1971. 'Food and feeding behaviour of Openbill Storks.' *Journal für Ornitologie.* 112:21-35.

KEAR, J. & DUPLAIX-HALL, N. 1975. *Flamingos.* Poyser, Berkhamsted.

KEITH, S., BENSON, C. W. & IRWIN, M. P. S. 1970. 'The genus *Sarothrura* (Aves: Rallidae).' *Bulletin of the American Museum of Natural History* 143.

LANGLEY, H. 1983. 'Biology of the Little Bittern in the south western Cape.' *Ostrich* 54:83-94.

LIVERSEDGE, T. N. 1980. 'A study of Pel's Fishing Owl *Scotopelia peli* Bonaparte 1850 in the "panhandle" region of the Okavango Delta.' Proceedings of the 4th Pan-African Ornithological Congress: 291-299.

MACLEAN, G. L. 1993. *Roberts' Birds of southern Africa.* John Voelcker Bird Book Fund, Cape Town.

MACLEAN, G. L. 1987. 'Seasonal changes in the birdlife of north-eastern Botswana.' *Bokmakierie* 39:109-111.

MACLEAN, G. L. 1990. *Ornithology for Africa.* University of Natal Press, Pietermaritzburg.

MCKINNEY, D. F., SIEGFRIED, W. R., BALL, I. J. & FROST, P. G. H. 1979. 'Behavioural specializations for river life in the African Black Duck (*Anas sparsa* Eyton).' *Zoologica. Tierpsychologie* 48:349-400.

MIDDELMISS, E. 1958. 'The Southern Pochard *Netta erythrophthalma*.' *Ostrich* supplement 2:1-34.

MILEWSKI, A.V. 1976. 'Feeding ecology of the Slaty Egret *Egretta vinaceigula*.' *Ostrich* 47:132-134.

MILSTEIN, P. LE S. 1975. 'The biology of Barberspan, with special reference to the avifauna.' *Ostrich* supplement 10.

MILSTEIN, P. LE S. 1979. 'The evolutionary significance of wild hybridisation in South African highveld ducks.' *Ostrich* supplement 13:1-48.

MILSTEIN, P. LE S. 1985. 'Nomadic waterfowl are vulnerable.' *Bokmakierie* 37:9-11.

MOCK, D.W. & MOCK, K.C. 1980. 'Feeding behaviour and ecology of the Goliath Heron.' *Auk* 97:433-448.

MOREAU, R. E. 1943. 'The Halfcollared Kingfisher (*Alcedo semitorquata*) at the nest.' *Ostrich* 15:161-177.

NEWMAN, K. B. (ED.) 1971. *Birdlife in Southern Africa*. Purnell, Cape Town.

NOBLE, R.G. & HEMENS, J. 1978. 'Inland water ecosystems in South Africa — a review of research needs.' *South African National Scientific Programmes Report* no. 34.

OATLEY, T. B. & PRYS-JONES, R. P. 1986. 'A comparative analysis of movements of southern African waterfowl (Anatidae), based on ringing recoveries.' *South African Journal of Wildlife Research* 16:1-6.

OGILVIE, M. & OGILVIE, C. 1986. *Flamingos*. Alan Sutton, Gloucester.

PIPER, S. E. 1989. 'Breeding biology of the Longtailed Wagtail *Motacilla clara*.' *Ostrich* supplement 14:7-15.

PIPER, S. E. & SCHULTZ, D. M. 1989. 'Type, dimensionality and size of Longtailed Wagtail territories.' *Ostrich* supplement 14:123-131.

PORTER, R. N. & FORREST, G.W. 1974. 'First successful breeding of Greater Flamingo in Natal, South Africa.' *Lammergeier* 21:26-33.

RIPLEY, D. 1977. *Rails of the world*. Godine, Boston.

ROWAN, M. K. 1963. 'The Yellowbill Duck *Anas undulata* Dubois in Southern Africa.' *Ostrich* supplement 5:1-56.

RYAN, P., UNDERHILL, L. G., COOPER, J. & WALTNER, M. 1988. 'Waders (Charadrii) and other waterbirds on the coast, adjacent wetlands and offshore islands of the southwestern Cape Province, South Africa.' *Bontebok* 6:1-19.

SIEGFRIED, W. R. 1965. 'The Cape Shoveller *Anas smithii* (Hartert) in southern Africa.' *Ostrich* 36:155-198.

SIEGFRIED, W. R. 1970. 'Wildfowl distribution, conservation and research in southern Africa.' *Wildfowl* 21:89-98.

SIEGFRIED, W. R., WILLIAMS, A. J., FROST, P. G. H. & KINAHAN, J. B. 1975. 'Plumage and ecology of cormorants.' *Zoologica Africana* 16:183-192.

SKEAD, D. M. & DEAN, W. R. J. 1977. 'Seasonal abundance of Anatidae at Barberspan.' *Ostrich* supplement 12:3-42.

SUMMERS, R. & WALTNER, M. 1979. 'Seasonal variations in the mass of waders in southern Africa with special reference to migration.' *Ostrich* 50:21-37.

TAYLOR, R. 1991. *The greater St Lucia wetland park*. Parke-Davis, Johannesburg.

TREE, A. J. 1978. 'A visit to Makgadikgadi Pan in April 1974.' *Honeyguide* 95:39-41.

TREE, A. J. 1987. 'Ringing recoveries and migration of Greenshank between Europe and Africa.' *Safring News* 16:51-66.

UNDERHILL, L. G. 1986. 'A successful breeding season for Brent Geese, Curlew Sandpipers and Sanderlings in 1985.' *Safring News* 15:15-18.

UNDERHILL, L. G. 1987. 'Waders (Charadrii) and other waterbirds at Langebaan Lagoon, South Africa, 1975-1986.' *Ostrich* 58:145-155.

UYS, C. J., BROEKHUYSEN, G. J., MARTIN, J. & MACLEOD, J. G. 1963. 'Observations on the breeding of the Greater Flamingo *Phoenicopterus ruber* Linnaeus in the Bredasdorp district, South Africa.' *Ostrich* 34:129-154.

VANDERWALLE, F. J. 1985. 'Combined canopy and foot-stirring functions in the Black Egret.' *Bokmakierie* 37:73-75.

WHITFIELD, A. K. & BLABER, S. J. M. 1979. 'Feeding ecology of piscivorous birds at Lake St Lucia, parts II and III.' *Ostrich* 50:1-20.

WILLIAMS, G. D., COPPINGER, M. P. & MACLEAN, G. L. 1989. 'Distribution and breeding of the Rock Pratincole on the upper and middle Zambezi River.' *Ostrich* 60:55-64.

WILLIAMS, J. 1987. 'Birding on the Zambezi River.' *Bokmakierie* 39:81-83.

WILSON, R.T. & WILSON, M. P. 1984. 'Breeding biology of the Hamerkop.' Proceedings of the 5th Pan-African Ornithological Congress: 855-865.

WOLFF, S.W. & MILSTEIN, P. LE S. 1976. 'Rediscovery of the Whitewinged Flufftail in South Africa.' *Bokmakierie* 28:33-36.

ZALOUMIS, E. A. & MILSTEIN, P. LE S. 1975. 'The conservation of wetland habitats for waterfowl in southern Africa.' *African Wildlife* supplement to 29, I.

Index

Page references in *italic* type denote photographs

137

LIST OF SUBSCRIBERS

SPONSORS' EDITION

Steve Bales

Angela Blanden

Jim Gerard Paul Broekhuysen

S. F. Cairns

Dr H. B. Dyer

Kathleen Satchwell

Struik Winchester

Collectors' Edition

A. J. Ardington

Don Barrell

P. A. Becker

Bevan Family

Colin Blythe-Wood

David K. Bond

The Brenthurst Library

S. W. Caroline

Elaine Cormack

R. M. Crawford

Dr & Mrs J. P. G. du Plessis

Professor P. K. Faure

Peter Ford

Eugene & Lalie Fourie

Richard & Barbara Galpin

E. S. C. Garner

Lydia Gorvy

Pat & Karin Goss

Adin & Sharon Greaves

I. H. Greenaway

John K. Hepburn

R. W. B. Hodgson

Barbara & Owen Hooker

C. R. Hunting

L. R. Hunting

M. S. Hunting

Malcolm Keeley

Rodd & Noreen Kippen

Helen Leibel

Micheline Logan

O. J. Mackenzie

Tian Mans

Kelly & Carol Manson

Nigel Matthews

Ian McCall

James McLuskie

M. S. Mullins

Jan & Elizabeth Nel

L-M Nicholls

Paul E. Norris

Dr -Ing. E. H. Kurt Obländer

Danie, Daniel & Christiaan Olivier

Ian Outram

John & Jeannine Pearse

J. Philip

Dr & Mrs D. G. C. Presbury

Peter G. S. Radford

Rodney K. Reynolds

Chris & Cathy Shaw

Jill & Mike Snaddon

Stocks Housing (Pty) Ltd

Brian Stott

Struik Winchester

M. L. & G. C. Sumner

Ian R. F. Trollip

G. H. Tudor

W. van Rÿswÿck

H. J. van Wyk

Fred & Adèle Vincent

Roy & Lorraine Webber

W. M. Wedderburn

Cathy & Henry Abrey
Gerald Ackerman
Graham Acutt
Africana Book Collectors
M. Alberts
Barry Alleson
David & Ann Alston
Annelise Andersen
Mr & Mrs D. J. Anderson
M. K. Angliss
Anglo American Coal Corporation
    Limited (Amcoal)
D. A. Arnott
P. G. Arnott
R. G. Arnott
G. A. Atkinson
John Austin & Margie Phipps

Ann Bailes
D. W. Bailey
Paoletta Baker
Gina Baldo
Roger & Audrey Baldwin
K. R. Baragwanath
Peter Barichievy
Norman E. C. Barlow
Don Barrell
E. A. Barry
Dr A. E. Bateman
David & Cathy Bath
Peter Bayly
Jane Bedford
Reinher H. Behrens
Ainsley John Bennett
Dr & Mrs R. M. F. Berard
Henry Bernitz
Prof. Gerhard J. Beukes
Coenraad Birkenstock
John E. Bishop
Dee & David Black

Michael & Cynthia Black
Hilton Blake
Cecil & Marian Bleksley
Anthony G. Bloomer
Arryn Blumberg
Ellen Bolding
Jeremy Bolton
Sarah, Caroline & Simon Borchert
Elizabeth Boshoff
Willem & Elfriede Boshoff
Rudolph Botha
John Bowen
Miles Bowker
L. G. Boyle
Edna & Frank Bradlow
Patrick Brett
Mimi Brian
Dave Brierley
Peter Brigg
Andrew Brink
Gordon & Penny Brodie
Michael Bromwich
Carole Brown
Prof. John M. M. Brown
Eric & Rae Bruce
N. R. G. Brunette
Sue Brunke
A. P. Bugden
Henri, Engela & Jacques Burger
A. N. Burkheiser
E. N. Burnett
Rob & Wendy Burnett
Terence Burns

Rupert Calcott
Alan Calenborne
Dr Camey
Kelson Camp
Dr Hamish A. Campbell
May & Gerald Carson

Michael, Geraldine & Richard Cassidy
Ann & Bryan Cawse
M. J. Challis
David & Margot Chamberlain
Peter Chrystal
C. J. Cilliers
A. H. Clarke
P. J. Clarke
A. C. V. Clarkson
Glenda Cleaver
Bruce Cloete
C. L. Clucas
P. L. B. Clucas
B. M. E. Coaton
Johann & Steph Coetzee
H. D. Conradie
Consol Ltd
Gael & Neville Constable
Peter & Carol Cook
C. L. Cousins
Llewellyn Crewe-Brown
Bob & Elenore Crosbie
Janette Cumming
Richard & Stephanie Cunliffe
Harold H. Currie
Kerry Curtis

Willem Daffue
Hillel Damelin
E. P. O. Dandrieux
N. O. Davies
Andrea & Candice Davison
Chris & Lynn Day
Jennifer Day
Sam & Ralda de Beer
C. J. & M. J. Dekker
F. B. de Kock
Margaret de Villiers
Gill Dewar
Helen Dewar

Janet Dewar
Marlene Dickerson
C. M. Dickson
W. S. Dougherty
Christopher du Cane
Francois du Randt
Bill & Jenny Duckworth
K. W. G. Duff
Graham Dumbrill
Margot, Ewen Duncan & Family
Janice Dunstan
Mrs J. Duursma
W. I. Duvenhage
Keith & Greer Dyer

Rob & Trudi Earle
Anne Edgecombe
Bill (E. A.) Edwards
Mike & Janine Egan
Cara Eksteen
Richard Eley
Roger & Sue Ellis
Arno Ellmer
Rodney Else
Barry Emberton
Ian & Janet Emmott
W. D. Erskine
H. P. Erwee
Dr I. B., Mrs A. H. & Miss G. L. Evans
M. G. Evans

Joe & Gwyn Faller
Pauline Farquhar
Trevor & Carol Fayers & Family
A. I. Ferguson
W. A. I. Ferguson
Mr & Mrs Nigel Fernsby
Khaki Ferreira
Peter B. Ferrett
Nicky Field
Isobel Forbes
Malcolm Foster
Beverley Fourie
Eugene & Lalie Fourie

Jan-Hendrik Fourie
Mrs Tineke Friederich
R. M. Fritz
Albert Froneman
M. R. Funston
Cathryn Futerman
Mike Fynn

J. A. Gardner
Francois & Karin Garrard
Niki Garratt
Michael Georgiou
Barrie & Pam Gibson
Alice Gilbert
Godfrey & Nicky Giles
Tony & Shane Girling
Margot & Patrick Glyn
Hubert & Diana Goetsch
Robin & Jill Goetsch
Ken Gordon
J. M. Gosnell
Kenneth Goulding
Dr & Mrs G. J. Greeff
Rod & Sue Green
M. E. A. Greenaway
Ronayne Greenshields
Bob & Marlene Griffin
Nico Grobbelaar
Adri Grobler
Mev. M. Eloff Grobler
John Groenewald
M. L. Guittard
A. H. Gunn

Helen Hahn
Anthony, Bernie, André & Tony Hall
Dorothy G. Hall
R. G. Halton
Dr Christopher A. Hammond
Mark B. Hardy
B. Harris
Eddie, Liz & Ansel Harris
R. Harris
R. A. Harvey

Ray & Julie Hattingh
Judith Hawarden
I. N. Hayward
Jon & Marje Hemp
Glynn & Anne Herbert
V. J. M. Hickman
Brian Colin Hodge
E. A. Hodgkinson
N. v. R. Hoets
Lex Hollmann Trust
Gordon Holtshausen
Diana Hood
Rupert & Nadia Horley & Family
Gwyn & Ted Horn
Geoffrey Marcus Howell
J. T. Hund
Ian B. Huntley

Joe & Jane Irvine

Antonie Jagga
Mimi Jansen
Andrew & Barbara Jay
R. F. Jeffery
Johannesburg City Library
Ralf Johannsen
Clive Scott Johnson
Jennifer Jones
Linda Jones
M. Jordaan
Ronél Jordaan
Inez Jordan
Marco & Michelle Josi
Paul A. M. Joubert
Joy Family

Mrs E. F. (Dinky) Kahn
Pamela Kaufman
Raymond E. Keeping
Anita Keevy
Clive & Aliki Kelly
Graeme Kendall
Mick Killeen
G. A. King

Donald B. Kinross
Mary Kirk
Johan & Koos Kloppers
Leon & Pauline Klugman
David Garth Knott
At & Elna Kotze
Ian Krawitz
Errol & Fredia Kreutzer
Keith & Germaine Krog
Franci & Mariaan Krone
Yvonne Kruger

R. Lambert
Neil Langley
Herb A. Larkan
P. J. Latham
R. M. Lawrie
Brett Lawson
Charles & Bev Leach
Dr Diane Carol Leach
Dr & Mrs A. R. Leask
C. J. le Cordeur
Le Quartier Français
Pierre & Sylvia le Roux
Reinhard & Emma le Roux
Allan H. Levin
Barry Lewis
J. M. Lewis
Linda Lewis
Andre P. Liebenberg
Edward B. L. Lightbody
Mr & Mrs A. J. M. Lind
Ian Hamilton Little
Lynton & Iris Lockwood-Hall
C. J. Loftus
Henk & André Loots
Felicity Louw
Peter & Gaynor Louw
David, Lesley, Warren & Jessica Luyt

Gordon Lindsay Maclean
K. M. V. Macwhirter
Y. M. Makda
Christian Manciot

Estee Rivka Mandelberg
John & Bev Manning
C. S. Manson
Riaan Marais
Ann & Bill Marklew
G. C. Marneweck
Olga & Bill Marsay
Audrey Marshall
P. Marshall
Robbie & Lyn Massey-Hicks
Brian R. Matthews
Heather K. McBurnie
Wendy E. McCallum
R. A. McClelland
Brian McDonald
Ron McDonald
Brian & Lynne McDonogh
Don Mc Dougall
Beryl McMenamin
D. B. Miller
D. M. Miller
J. K. Miller
Wendy & John Milton
David B. Mitchell
John Molyneux Carter
S. L. Moorcroft
Patrick Morant
Jill Mortimer
Wenda Mould
C. L. Mowat
René & Elmarie Mulder
Bryce Munro
Neil Munro
Gareth Wright Murray

David Nabarro
Bruce & Cilla Nel
Jan & Elizabeth Nel
Anne & Peter Nelson
Pam & Bill Nicol
Mrs G. A. Nikschtat
Janet Norman & Sean Longhurst
Roy James Norman
Gilly & Bambi Notten

Eric Eugene Nutt
Rick Nuttall

Dr Pam Oberem
Adrian Ogilvie
T. M. Ogilvie Thompson
Alida & Peter Oldroyd
Mrs Rhona Oxlee

John Pallett
Timothy J. Partridge
Dr I. M. Patz
Alan F. Payne
Keith S. Peacock
Geoff & Jenny Peatling
Anne, Belinda, Carolyn & Anthony Peepall
Jeffry Perlman
Noel & Audrey Peverett
Rodney Lionel Phillips
Dr A. J. & Mev. Pienaar
Johanna Pistorius
Rosemarie Ploger
Kevin & Glynis Podmore
George & Penny Poole
Ferdinand Postma Library, Potch. Univ. for CHE
Fritz & Karin Potgieter
Jeanne A. Potgieter
Lt. Col. G. K. M. Potts
Quentin Pretorius
Walter Prozesky
Dr P. J. Pullinger

Gordon Radcliffe
Fred & Martie Ramsay
Muhammad Ilyaas Randeree
Patti & Bernard Ravnö
Anita Redelinghuys
Pamela Redtenbacher
W. A. C. Reniers
Neil Richards
G. V. C. Richardson
Johann Rissik
Alec Shepherd Roberts
Cecily Roberts
Douglas Roberts

N. G. Roberts

Sean C. Roberts

David Robertson

C. Robinson

Cedric Roché

Eva Roehl

Rolfes Bernhard

G. E. S. Ronaldson

C. J. Roos

Z. A. Rossouw (Dr)

Alexander Rowe

Neville Rowe

Errol Sackstein

Ken Sandison

Con en Jacqueline Schabort

Hein Scheepers

Albert Schultz

G. E. Scott-Ronaldson

W. G. Scurr

Robert William Semple

Di Sendin

David Shapiro

Sylvia & Bernard Shull

J. F. K. Sievers

Willy, Wendy, Robert & Liza Simon

Cecil & Thelma Skotnes

Ansie & Dennis Slotow

Mr & Mrs Leon Slotow

F. C. Smart

Keith & Dorothy Smith

Mariette A. Smith

Dr S. A. Smith (Snr)

S. A. Smith (Jnr)

Michiel & Morag Smuts

Peter Smuts

Carol & Chris Soames

Ronald Sourgen

Natalie Southwood

I. J. J. Spangenberg

Sarel Spies

Wald & Lilla Stack

S. A. H. Statham

Rob & Ané Stegmann

Robert Stein

J. Stemmett

Gideon F. Steyn

Peter & Elsa Street

Sandy Stretton

Diana & David Stride

Pieter Struik

Terri & Jolene Stupel

P. R. Sumner

Quentin Sussman

Eric & Fiona Sutton

Ina Svoboda

Mike Swartz

Prof. M. B. E. Sweet

Takis Family

O. J. Taylor

Vincent & Pam Taylor

Colin & Ann Tedder

Dr Walther Thiede

Bea Tindall

Jennifer Tinkler

Dr & Mrs P. A. Tonkin

Craig Tooley

Treehaven Waterfowl Trust

Stefan Triegaardt

Alroy Trout

Stewart & Colleen Tucker

Harvey Tuckett

Glynn Tudor

M. Twentyman-Jones

Dr A. C. van Bruggen

D. L. van Coller

Leonie van den Berg

Aat & Thea van der Dussen

Dick & Liz van der Jagt

Chris & Corrie van der Linde

Dr John Vandermade

Francois van der Merwe

J. J. van der Merwe

Paul & Gerda van der Reyden

Nicolaas van Doesburgh

J. F. van Gass

Robbert van Oosterhout

Cecilia van Rensburg

J. J. van Rensburg

Malan van Rensburg

M. & M. A. van Rijswijck

Chris van Rooyen

C. R. van Rooyen

Philip van Rooyen

Dr M. C. E. van Schoor

Marius & Lenette van Wyk

Helm & Gill van Zijl

Gigi van Zyl

Leon & Elise Venter

M. J. S. Verhaart

Verlorenvlei Country Inn

T. G. Vetten

Graham & Milly Vickers

Fred & Adele Vincent

Attie Visser

Willie & Joan Vlok

M. von Fintel

Eric von Glehn

Ronald Wainwright

Rex & Ethne Wakely-Smith

Binnie Walker

Pat & Jim Wallace

Wally Walters

Alex & Elaine Watson

Prof. Ian B. Watt

Roy & Lorraine Webber

Ilse & Stephan Wentzel

Hon. Louis Weyers

Gill Wheeler

Wheldon & Wesley Ltd.

Jill & Alan Whyte

Dietmar Wiening

Jean Wilson

Robert & Bobbie Wise

Dr G. S. Withinshaw

B. Nigel Wolstenholme

Mark Wood

E. J. Woodcock

Rita Wright

Sponsors' and Collectors' Editions bound by Peter Carstens, Johannesburg